WITH FAMILY HELP

Carl Rooney

CONTENTS

FOREWORD

My Uncle Tom gave me the first push I needed to write this story without realising it, by saying, "You'll need a ghost writer." Not if I DO IT MYSELF, I thought, and then I'll ask my genius uncle to help polish the book up a bit to make it more readable. Uncle Tom was a genius, and I knew he could refine my writing enough to publish. Unfortunately, my dear uncle passed before I finished my first draft but I made up my mind to continue, so I asked my Uncle Phil to help me, and he did.

I do hope that this photographic self-help book helps others with physical limitations.

PROLOGUE

Not at all academic, I feel I have a far more creative soul. As a photographer, I often see the beauty in the simplest things.

"Never stop believing in HOPE because miracles happen every day." Now here's a quote I loved from the first minute I saw it.

NOTE TO MY READERS

Inception – Here are just a few of the things I have learned from self-help books and radio that helped inspire me to write something that might help others.

1) Oprah Winfrey was badly abused as a child, but now she is financially comfortable and helps others. She doesn't have children herself as she is too career-minded. But because of that, she's been able to help hundreds (maybe thousands) more.

2) In the Auschwitz Concentration Camps, prisoners all thought there was no way out until one man asked, "How can I escape this camp?" Repeatedly being told, "You can't escape," he chose not to believe it was impossible and he managed to escape.

3) And this, something that had never crossed my mind before. Why do some men cry their eyes out at a football game if their team loses, even though their team will play again the following week? (Definitely a conundrum, that one!)

And now, I'd like to welcome you into my mind and heart.

First, I thank each of you who have decided to read this book of thoughts, ideas, and stories of my journeys around the world. My journaling of random thoughts and memories started as something to help me remember what a good life I have led, regardless of my disability. But once I got started, I realised what a cathartic effect writing about my life had on me. Instead of pitying myself, I remembered all the wonderful places I had been and all the people I had met throughout my life. Looking back, I realised I'd had an uncanny ability to make people feel better about themselves. One way I did that was mentoring children when I was a Camp Counsellor.

Please know that this recounting of some of my life's experiences and thoughts has been jotted down in random order as I tend to jump ahead and then back again. That's just how my thought process works!

I hope that these thoughts and snippets from my life profoundly affect you as they did me. My wish is for you to find peace and happiness in your life, to realise the best part of you, and impart your kindness and wisdom to others who may need it, oftentimes more than anyone can see or know.

CHAPTER 1: IN THE BEGINNING

I was born on a Thursday at 3:45 P.M. on the 26th of February in 1984 in England, which comparatively, is a wealthy country. I did not choose this; it just happened. I can only assume I entered the world headfirst, screaming, as most babies do, although I can't claim to remember it.

For most of my life, I've enjoyed waking up by taking a big four-limb-stretch and then splashing my face with cold water twice (or even thrice) in the bathroom sink. The cold water does shock you into waking up.

I vaguely remember a time when I was about four when I must have embarrassed my Mum, although maybe she just got a good laugh. Four-year-olds are known for their curiosity and I remember looking around as Mum and I strolled through a church to a chessboard. About halfway through, I stopped and suddenly looked up at a priest and asked, "Are you a human bean?" I wonder what the priest and my Mum thought about that coming from the mouth of a four-year-old.

Another of my earliest memories is being in my English Nan's garden, in a corner, aiding with the gardening. Actually, at that age and me just about birdbath height, I could not have done much. After that day, I became a great little worker.

A little later at primary school, waiting in the dinner queue, I misheard something and answered, "Sorry, what?" This kid roughly my age snapped at me and said, "You do not say what, you say pardon!" A strange thing to remember, from way back in 1989.

My beautiful Sister and me, in Skerries, Ireland.

When I was young, I'm not sure why, but every time I went to sit down on the toilet, I always felt the need to remove my jumper, T-shirt, whatever! I was completely naked. I have heard a lot of children do this. Why? I don't know. It's a bit odd when I think about it now.

At a parent's evening, there was a P.E. (physical education) teacher in hysterics because of an answer to a question I had been given. What is a balanced diet made up of? I hadn't a clue but thought it best not to leave it blank. So, I wrote fifty-percent of good things and fifty-percent of bad things. I had just reached secondary school and thought it was a good guess. I mean, that's balanced, isn't it?

People say that when I burped, I would hiccup and fart simultaneously, and I recall playing the guitar on my one-eyed Willy (aka penis) quite often. You would think I would be a natural at the guitar in later life; I wasn't. I was an imaginative child, so perhaps I was wondering why my snake wasn't longer!

Occasionally, I have this vague memory of being in the primary school hall, sitting cross-legged on the floor, awaiting our P.E. class to begin, and a tennis ball coming at us from overhead. I instantly raised my arm to let the ball land in my hand, and as soon as it did, my fingers very quickly closed around the ball. I could hear most of the class cheering; I'd caught it!

While growing up, I always had a fear of river edges and falling in. Even into my late teenage years, I used to wonder what's wrong with me. Of course, friends and family have always said there was nothing wrong with me.

I was eleven years old, and I went camping with Neil, a good friend, in their back garden for a night. I was not comfortable and decided to go home. Fortunately for me, my friend's Dad brought me back home around 12:30 A.M. Oh well, these things happen. I must have been scared, or maybe just frightened by a strange sound.

On another weekend with this same friend, we made window shutters with a piece of string and transparent Perspex in our own little den. We were only eleven. Suddenly, a downpour came from nowhere, and we got proper soaked, so much for the Perspex windows. At least we tried and succeeded until the downpour came.

My sister Shehrina had two pet rats growing up, bizarrely named Bill & Ben (after the flower pot men: the animated sunflowers in pots from back in the '60s). Soon we would be going to a Center Parcs holiday, and not thinking, I asked Mum whether we had bought tickets for the rats to go on holiday too. Silly ole' me.

Oh well, life goes on, doesn't it? We all make mistakes, drop things, spill drinks, and even break things accidentally. It doesn't matter anyhow; you can either fix it, mop it up, shout "Oh damn!" and hopefully, we pay more attention next time. This is how everyone learns – through their mistakes. Everybody needs space and what you do with that space is up to you.

As I slowly grew up, I did not know why I was here and

often wondered about that. It was only when I was in my early thirties when suddenly, I realised I was put here to help others who are less fortunate than me and perhaps ease their suffering.

I found one way I can feel better about bad things happening to me is to give them as little attention as possible. For example, if it is cold outside, you shouldn't think of the cold; otherwise, you'll feel the cold. And if you hurt yourself, the more you think about the pain, the more it will hurt. If you forget something, the more you think about it, you may get frustrated and then possibly angry and start blaming others. If you get into an altercation, the best thing to do is to back down and sort things out nicely like adults some other day. If you cannot, leave the room quietly and have a quiet discussion another time, respectfully, as adults should do. The more you look at the clock or a watch, the slower the time goes. I first figured that one out in Physics class in secondary school because the teacher was very boring.

No matter if the weather gives you snow, rain, or sunshine, you must always find a way to be positive and happy. Having a positive attitude will cause others around you to be more positive and that will spread your happiness all around.

I absolutely love travelling. Each time I would leave my homeland, I would always be delighted. I suppose I caught the so-called 'travel bug' at a young age. I am happy I travelled when I was young because travelling is not easy for me now, though I still consider myself young. Mum used to say, "You're as young as you feel."

My mother and her partner are avid listeners of LBC Radio (a London based broadcasting station). It's more of a chat station where you phone in to have a moan. I like the fact it is keeping me abreast of current affairs. It's annoying when you have people saying, "I don't like saying that I am British in airports now!" In my mind, I thought, well then, don't mention you're British! (Like you can get away with not showing your ID everywhere like that now!)

Honestly, saying you're happy is an easy thing to do. Even if you are quite unhappy, listen to people, take their advice, and you will change without thinking. Because when you are happy, life becomes so much easier and you start thinking of ways to make others happy too, which is a very good thing.

When I was young, and an adult referred to a child splitting their head open, I used to picture that as falling into two halves. Also, being told about electric cables, I wondered why birds could just hop on and off of them so freely. I hadn't grasped an understanding of the earth wire yet.

You learn many things at school, including some things you do not wish to learn, I wish I'd known this while I was still in school instead of later! Do not concern yourself with things like this. Do as you are told and avoid getting in trouble at school because it is inevitable that you'll leave school one day. So, it is best to learn as much as you can while at school, as it becomes harder to retain information when you get older.

Many people have hidden disabilities, too. Things you can't see, although maybe you hear about it. But I don't ever judge by those things because I believe our abilities, not our disabilities, define us.

It was also a massive shock when I heard in Leonardo Di Caprio's documentary film, "Before the Flood" that approximately three-hundred-thousand people in India live without electricity. I find that a crying shame as it is now 2017, and I am thirty-three-years-old. Why didn't I learn this in school so I could try and do something to help these people? Strange, the things they forget to teach us.

What do we learn at school! The one thing I clearly remember from school is a business teacher being asked in the sixth form (by a seventeen-year-old), "Oi, sir, who do you support?" Expecting a top league football team, he just quietly answered, "My wife and kids." The class was in stitches laughing but as I got older, I realised just how true that statement was.

I can also vaguely recall some long, exhausting, cross-country running. There must have been benefits to going to school. The social interactions must have helped, with students and teachers alike. I can recall being nearly kicked off my chair in a woodworking class once. I was a timid boy. Was that necessary? No, it certainly wasn't; it just left me terrified of the teacher. I came away without having learned a thing in that class I could use later in life. Everyone is different – perhaps you found school very informative, but many others share an opposite opinion.

One good thing about school was the French class. I say that only because I seemed to be one of the top three pupils in the class since I was eleven-years-old. My great grandfather on my mother's side was a Frenchman, perhaps that was why I had a flair for French and other languages. As I moved into adulthood, it is inevitable everyone is going to make mistakes. That is how we learn as human beings. It is how we react to our mistakes-what we learn from them- that matters.

My six-year-old niece threw a horrendous tantrum when I beat her at a game of chess. She was screaming and kicking. It was quite sad to see. When she finally calmed down, she sat, and I gently told her that it is okay to lose. It is not the end of the world; we can always play again. Life goes on whether we win at something or lose, and remember, there's always another chance. In the last two years, this niece has learned that it is not essential to win all the time. Even though it is necessary to go into games set on winning, otherwise, know that you may well lose. Just don't think about it; just be sure to do your absolute best.

At the age of eleven, while at Cub Scouts, we played a game but I have forgotten the name of it. It was fun though. We played it in a small, rectangular room with two chairs on either side of the room, two children, each with a rope, stood on the chairs facing each other. We would swing into the middle of the room and try to get the other child to let go of the rope and fall to the floor. When it was my turn, I was able to stay on the rope until it stopped swinging. That was when it became tough, as I didn't want to lose. Children around us, shouting, "Just hang on." We hung there for three to five minutes, but I could see the other child was about to give up. In the end, I slowly slid to the ground, and I lost. Did that loss make a difference in my life? Of course not. Perhaps psychologically, it helped me become the persistent chap I am today; a person who never gives up.

Everyone has their own unique story to tell, and everyone has their own individual abilities. I used to have a bilateral tremor in my upper arm. I hated the class dictations that happened every few weeks. Though I was a good speller, it was tough for me to steady my arm during dictations. I often used to leave blank spaces and come back and fill them in at the end of the dictation. The one misspelling I can recall was the word 'able,' I had spelled it 'abel.' At the time, I was displeased because I got nineteen out of twenty correct. I had spent ages revising for this test.

I truly believed I would get all twenty right. Oh well, what a pity, how sad, never mind.

One thing is for sure. It is really helpful to live by a routine. This will allow you time to make daily plans, and in a strange, kind of subliminal way, it gives you more time as well. Planning is a very positive thing to practice, no matter what age you are. As long as you are well aware, there are only twenty-four hours in a day.

At the age of eighteen, following a photography class, I decided to type a letter (with family help) and get it faxed off to various fashion designers who would participate in the London Fashion Week. Fortunately, from the forty or so faxes my Mum thankfully sent, I received three positive answers. That meant I had three invitations to the London Fashion Week show. If I hadn't tried, I would have never known I could get any invitations at all.

The world is an amazing place, and travel is important; you will learn things that are not taught in the school system. Just today (17/01/2018), while waiting for an appointment in Charing Cross Hospital, London, I was patiently awaiting Mum in the loo (toilet) while people watched the swarms of people around them. It isn't often you hear this, but you've heard of bird watching and whale watching quite often. Through travelling you can do these things along with dolphin swimming, gorilla trekking, or even eagle spotting. I think getting in touch with nature makes you a better person.

When you're unwell, you get better faster if you are a positive person or an optimistic thinker. It is a strange thing, but I was eleven-years-old when I first realised that continually thinking of the pain only makes it linger. If you cut or injure yourself, the faster you stop dwelling on the pain, the faster the pain goes away.

Why is it that when the weather gets cold, we become moodier than usual and stay indoors watching repeats on TV or the News that is on a loop every fifteen minutes? Unfortunately, it is mostly negative. "Na, I don't want to go to my Pilates class; it's cold outside." I do not get that. Why possibly injure yourself by skipping class just because it is too cold? What are coats for?

You can fail at something you don't even want. Be it a job, a game, or a race, so you may as well take a chance and do something you love or at least enjoy. Do more of what makes you happy. A gym is an excellent place for a lot of people to start. Exercise is extremely important, and gyms are social places. You could make friends, or even meet your future wife or husband there.

So much of life is a blur when you're a child, and for many of us, our memories fade rather quickly, the more exciting things we do. "Keyan, stop wasting the sellotape, or there will be none left!" At five, you don't really expect this, "Yeah, Uncle Carl, we can buy some more sellotape."

In the same year, still being the same five-year-old, we were in Bella Italia, our local restaurant. "Grandpa, are we having starters?" Uncle Carl had not even heard of this word until, at least twelve years of age. Uncle Carl's response went something like this, "The next thing ya know, you'll have babies wanting to be driven around in only Ferrari's."

There does need to be more boot camps to discipline children and perhaps in a Latin American nation or an African nation and in a way that doesn't work in wealthy nations."

I do think many of us realise life is pretty hard after school, college, or University. Lots of people fall into the wrong relationship and have children, and end up doing a job they don't like just to make ends meet and put food on the table. Five years later, they find out they have studied the wrong thing and do whatever their parents recommend. We are all born as equals; it is what we choose to do in life that gets so many of us in a pickle.

Life is a wonderful thing; it is crucial to know the difference between right and wrong. We should all learn this at a young age. But do not be afraid to break the rules and take risks in life. If you make an error, so what? Just tweak it or try something else you enjoy. Do not give up trying to make a positive change to yourself and the world we live in. Start with a smile for others, and if you do not receive a smile back, it is not the end of the world. There will be somebody else to smile at and you can try again.

The internet came to life in the year 1990, and a couple of years later, we had the smartphone. Though for me, I didn't get my first smartphone until early 2014. Then a few years later came the very popular DVD. Technology is forever changing and improving. Computers never interested me; so, if something does not interest you, do not do it. Definitely do not start a job in the hopes of becoming rich. Being rich certainly does not make you happy, especially if you are in a job you don't like and have to do it day in and day out.

I was around eight or nine years of age and was with my Dad and sister. Before getting suited up to play Quasar, my Dad thought it would be funny to write his name as Mickey Mouse. What he did not realise was that the name list was going to be checked and moments later a youngish chap asked, "Where's Mickey Mouse, can you write your name correctly please?" It made my sister, and me laugh, which was the main reason I still have this memory, I suppose.

Once upon a time, while in Dublin, Ireland with Dad, we were climbing Mount Sugarloaf. I wanted to go a certain way down; I suppose I thought it would be quicker and easier. I vaguely remember flipping or doing a forward roll when I was not meant to. After shouting back to my Dad and stepmom in pain, he just said something like, "Well, you did choose to go that way. We did tell you!" Nobody came to my aid, so I hobbled down alone. They possibly thought I was kidding around. I was about eleven-years-old, and it wasn't a joke!

"I think, therefore I am" is a famous quote by Rene Descartes, a French Philosopher or 'Je pense, donc Je suis,' first appearing in his 1637 book, *Discourse on the Method*. This phrase is still used today. Crazy, huh? That was such a long time ago to still be used in the world today.

I can recall my grandfather saying that "If everything was easy, son, everyone would do it," which is very true, yet most people moan and complain about how they dislike their job. There is no need for this; be grateful you have a job if you have one. If you do not like it, then leave and look for something you do like to do.

My six-year-old nephew claimed his one-year-old sister was very cute and then said, "That's why I like her." What's important to remember is we were once all children. Even adults say the wrong things without thinking, and they end up apologising shortly afterward.

One thing that is important to remember is that no one owes us a thing. We are all born equal and have control over our own lives. Whatever it is that you want to do, you must knowingly work hard to get it and believe you can get it. There may be a few errors along the way, which everybody goes through. But if you're tenacious, you'll get there.

People just do not realise that if you are nice to someone, that person will be nice to you in return, most times. If you are kind to someone, that person will be kind to you. If you are positive toward someone, then they will be positive toward you. If you hang around fitness people, then you may well become as fit as they are. If you hang around people who moan a lot, you will find you will start moaning yourself.

August 1999- Growing up, this is me about to climb
Mount Sugarloaf (Dublin, Ireland, Not Rio, Brazil)
while visiting my Dad over a summer holiday.

My life and your life are always shorter than you think. Just think the population has been growing for millions of years. As children, it is near impossible to understand that, in fact, you can't. We all grow up, make big mistakes along the way, even if we do our best. We get old, then go in and out of hospitals, then pass on. That is, as they say, 'The Circle of Life' – every living thing goes through this cycle. All the sea creatures, trees, plants, and animals. Anyway, if you think about it, no one would want to live forever. I think it would become a tad boring.

I think many people on earth take themselves far too seriously. These people have children, and once again, they raise them far too seriously and maybe read ten or more books on how to be a great Mum or Dad. The thing is, there is no one way to be a great parent, and while reading the author's opinion, you are just confusing yourself.

We all think uniquely; it's what divides us into different aspects of life. Those brave enough to escape the constant rubbish in the news, social media, or on the TV are heading in the right direction. Reading is very important; believing everything you read is a mistake. Listening to the wrong type of thing, believing it, then spreading this false information is also a mistake. Learning to speak and read more than one language is very important and may come in handy in later life.

What you read in papers may well be far from the truth. On social media, these days, one thing pops up, then another one shows up saying something else. Who should we believe? My advice is to sit on the fence and come to your own conclusion. It's silly sharing news that may very well be a lie. Be patient, listen, and then make up your own mind. Spreading something we aren't sure of just adds more confusion!

It is so easy to forget if you see a hot singer, a dancer, or the Queen, that they are humans, no different from you. They pee and poo like everyone else and go through life the same as we do. It's just that they have different jobs that allow them to be on the television.

The word 'famous' seems to have been blown out of proportion. For example, actors are no happier than we are and it is just their job that makes them famous and gets them on the TV. Have you seen these humanitarian adverts where they ask you to donate £2 or £3? I very much doubt these poor children or their families get paid a penny. But if you are an experienced actor from a wealthy country, then you will be paid millions. To me and many I know, it does seem very unfair.

July 2002- impressive Eiffel Tower (in the distance)

This was a quirky me who would rather do things outside the box. My Dad took me on a weekend trip to Paris. I started to grow bodily hair everywhere. Anyhow, most of you know that Paris is a romantic, architectural, and very picturesque place. I was sixteen years old, so I still had much to learn. The main focus point is in the distance between the trees.

Funny thing, human life. When it is freezing cold, people

complain about the weather. "It's miserable," my English Nan once groaned in the wind and mild, sporadic rainfall. But when there is a heatwave, again, people complain about the weather. I was working in Dublin Airport with Dad, and I heard from Dad that a plane load of Israelis came to Dublin every summer because of the inclement (bad) weather. That seemed like a weird thing to me.

The best way to go is to try and be as positive as much as possible. I know it is hard, but I also know that anything is possible. You just have to make an effort and try. You will find that through positivity, you become happier without thinking about it. Even a simple smile at a stranger can make someone's day.

Hearing or seeing the word 'No,' doesn't mean it's the end; it means 'Never stop believing in yourself' as others do, enjoy living life, and be happy. Volunteering and helping other people is a good starting block. It is hard for me to put into words, but you're already doing a wonderful thing by helping others. During my time spent in Uganda and painting the outside of a school's brick wall, I bizarrely found joy in making funny faces at the children in the class. The students found it funny. Their teacher called me in, so I played a game; surprisingly for me some of the Ugandan children knew 'Simon Says.' It was just as fun for me as it was for all thirty children.

I think when I was a young lad with Dad and the Irish family when we were in the car, my sister and I used to amuse ourselves playing a game we made up between us called 'that's my house.' This was in the late 1980s, a time when the internet didn't exist. There would often be shouting "Overtake!" while driving along on the dual carriageway. It's a bit different now, though, as many children play with tablets (portable computers) which are used to keep them occupied. They do kind of keep you entertained, which can keep children quiet and maybe keep the driver from having a crash. Unfortunately, this also can allow children to get an addictive nature. I say, just do not have kids, leaving you with a much happier life. Well, actually, I used to want to have two children of my own. Something happened later in life though, that made me decide not to have children. My sister had four children after being informed by the medical field she couldn't have any.

Every individual has their own story to tell. Hopefully, after reading this book, you'll come away with something useful that will change your own life for the better.

As I am sure you all know, each and every one of us has his or her own life to live. It is how we choose to live it that makes a huge difference. Living a positive, healthy path is the right path to choose. It does not matter what age you are; you can always choose to change direction and lead a happy life.

No one knows how life started, although some scientists may say otherwise. It is important to remember that we are here, and life isn't easy for anyone. The most important thing for achieving a fulfilling life is how we choose to live our lives and be happy with our decisions.

There are those people who bravely go to war for you and me and everyone else. These people are not superhuman; they have no special powers; they are just like everyone else and the other readers of this book. This has been the same all throughout history in the Battle of the Somme, Dunkirk, in fact, every war.

This is an amazingly sublime place, near to the Grand Canyon.

While on holiday with Dad in Phoenix, Arizona, we were on a horse trail on a hot, sunny, summer day. Soon after, we had a tub of ice cream. When I tasted it, I openly said it was cold. Dad found this hilarious. Because if ice cream isn't cold, it melts. I was seventeen-years-old – what a daft thing to say at that age. Oh well, we live and learn.

The photograph below was taken shortly before the ice cream incident.

This is not something I would do again. Horses are beautiful, but I'd much rather have my feet on the ground.

No photo in the world can do justice to the beauty of the Grand Canyon. Here's the best I could do, Taken just after take-off in a sightseeing helicopter.

*This photo is not too far from where I visited in Glendale, Arizona. Incredibly, **look at the size of that cactus**; I am about 180 cm or 5 ft 11 in. Words cannot describe the sheer size of it like this photograph of me next to it can!*

I find it crazy when seeing extremely muscular men and women in their briefs or bikinis appearing on occasional TV adverts or in newspaper ads. Their incredible-looking physique makes me forget that they are human too. Same with watching the gymnastics at the Olympics. They wee and poo and groan at having constipation as we all do. It's strange how quickly we forget that we all came into this world the same way as every other baby. Yes, we most certainly did. I think it is just a part of life, and it happens to everyone. With time, our memories fade. As of yet, we haven't remedied this one. I know it will be beyond my lifetime if we ever do.

Mum, sis, and I went to say goodbye to someone at London's Heathrow Airport; I forget who it was. A Scottish lady approached Mum and asked for directions. Mum has never been a great listener and replied quickly, "Oh, sorry, I don't speak French."

I do wonder why we are created the way we are. Obviously, we would look quite strange, all walking around with eight legs. What I meant by the first sentence was why our brains work the way they do and lead our emotions to operate the way they do. We still have no control over this.

I recently heard that teenage couples sometimes physically fight. Why? I do not know. As I had mentioned in the previous paragraph, we have no control over how our brains work. Human beings are uniquely different, capable of doing extraordinary things, but things take time, such as curing the many diseases out there.

My sixth form leader told me in 2001 that I would be the one boy this year who would not receive a recommendation for the UCAS University application form. There were sixty-six boys in that year group, and when I asked, "why?" I was told I do not listen, and I am not organised. I was still quite a shy kid so I did not dare argue. I suppose I did not see the point, as I was never going to win.

CHAPTER 2: BECOMING AN ADULT

I was a young boy of just four-years-old when my very loving parents got divorced, and my older sister and I had no idea why. Well, it was news to me.

I grew up a timid boy, visiting my Dad in Dublin during the holidays. While my sister, who was two years older than me, was much more of an extrovert, I was the opposite, very much an introvert. Even growing up I often wondered why I am here on earth.

My older sister constantly complained because I had the larger bedroom, and she quite often would stick her fingers up at me, then shout, "Mum! Carl stuck his fingers up at me." I never did, but Mum would always side with her, and this amused my sister. I guess many women are a lot more likely to side with their daughters, even if they know they are in the wrong. Perhaps it is a protective thing between women and girls.

This next thing is something I know I mentioned in Chapter One, but this memory has burnt itself into my psyche as something that really hurt. Oh, I was pissed off too, but mostly I hurt because I had studied so hard and I should have gotten every word in this test right. I was probably around eleven or twelve at the time. I studied really hard when I knew they would be giving those dictation spelling tests and I was a good speller. But an upper arm tremor made some things harder to do. The teacher would only pause for three or four seconds between the spelling test words, and my hand started shaking uncontrollably near the end. I got nineteen out of twenty; I had spelled the word 'able' wrong. I spelled it "abel." Once I started shaking, I couldn't think about the words. I have never forgotten how disappointed in myself and angry at everything I was after this experience. Why did I have to have that damn tremor? As I am sure you can tell, that experience has left its mark.

I can remember another time in secondary school; again, I must have been eleven or twelve. We were talking amongst ourselves about the names of our siblings. It was Majid's turn to speak. "I've got three brothers named Sajid, Dajid, and Wajid." The class erupted in laughter; I do not think I saw the funny side, to be honest. But, being in an explosion of laughter, I thought I should laugh too, so I would not seem to be the odd one out.

At about fourteen years of age, in Ireland with Dad, step-mum, and brother, I was playing on some sand dunes, not sure how but I can remember running into a wall of solid sand. Extremely painful, it was. I must have been running too fast and was unable to stop myself.

Around this time, my big sis and I would love to go to Ireland to see Dad and family, who would spoil us both rotten. Our first job was cleaning scallions (spring onions) at 4p a bunch, which was very stingy on the eyes and filthy dirty under the nails. We would sit down with twenty to thirty scallions on our laps, surrounded by crates of scallions, so there were always plenty to clean. It was the family's way of teaching us about money.

My Uncle Tom and me in front of the shed in Skerries

The long thin island you can see in the picture is Shenick Island which is roughly a mile from the shore. When the tide goes out, you can walk to this island. But once you get out there, you certainly have to be wary of the tide coming in.

In the summers that followed, I used to work at Dublin Airport with Dad. I used to board the flights. One Easter holiday, while getting off a flight from London to Dublin, I was met by my father and taken to his office to help load the next flight. I wasn't even asked. It was more like, 'we are very short-staffed; go and help the loaders.' I was only sixteen. I suppose it wasn't the end of the world.

When I would visit with my Dad, he often asked when he picked me up from Dublin Airport, "Do you wanna go straight home, or do you wanna go to the pub (licking his lips and growling) for a pint and then go home?" Once, after my third pint of beer, I vomited in front of everyone while dashing to the toilet. We immediately left after a quick tinkle before going home.

Anyway, I decided to stay on and do my A levels in Photography, French, Drama, and Computers. At the time, sadly for me, there was a clash in the timetable, so I had to drop one of the subjects. Computers had been the obvious choice as I wasn't overly interested. Probably should have thought if I can get a job in computers, I would be able to work my way up the career ladder to make a decent living and make an excellent income. At the time, though, that had not crossed my mind. To me, being stuck behind a computer all day to make a living sounds a bit tedious. At seventeen-years-old, I remember one of my photography teachers telling me I would never get a photography job as I was too shy. "We'll see!" I silently thought to myself.

For my final project, which was given to us shortly after 9/11 (11th of September, 2001) in America, we were asked to choose an issue. Not surprisingly, the majority in the class decided to cover 'War' for their project. Not being into any form of violence and believing war to be a terrible thing, I choose 'Fashion' for my project.

My completed Fashion Project

I drafted a letter, had my uncle polish it, and then asked Mum to fax it from her work to thirty-to-forty London Fashion Designers. Fortunately, I received four or five replies.

I went alone to London Fashion week and really enjoyed the experience. At one of these events, while everyone was gently munching on the hors d'oeuvres, I looked to my left and noticed I was standing next to Zoe Wanamaker, a British television and film actress. Recently I had seen her on the tele, strange, huh?

I recall a time in an English pub in Slough with Dad, sis and her boyfriend, and five or six other mates unknown to me. Dad leans across the table and just asks the boyfriend, "Are ya fuckin' me daughter?" That's my 'no shame' Dad, clearly doesn't think before he speaks; not the sharpest tool in the shed. The level of intelligence your parents have does not matter.

As I was nearing eighteen-years-old, I was in a school workshop when I had heard about a gap year commission in the army paying £10,000 if you give them ten months of your time. Because of this, I joined the after-school rugby club to improve my fitness, bizarrely (because I wasn't used to it) receiving a lot more respect from the school senior prefects. I was only doing 1 A Level and 2 A/S's, which I was told is equivalent to an A-Level. I found this was not the case when I saw an Army Careers advisor in Chippenham. I wasn't academic enough to do the Army Gap Year Commission. Oh well, these things happen! In the summer holidays, I worked with my Dad at Dublin Airport. He was a dispatcher and knew his boss fairly well, which meant at the time, 1999, I didn't even have to interview. Great huh?

A year later, I had a boss, 'Marc' something. A French chap who told me the best way to learn a language is to live in the country of the specific language and surround yourself with the language. He suggested trying to work in Disneyland Paris to improve my French. That way, you force yourself to learn. When

I returned home to England, I wrote three handwritten letters and emailed twice to Disneyland Paris. Seven long months later, patiently waiting, I was invited for an interview in London. Delighted, I was. It's 2001, on a train with Mum to somewhere in London for the interview. Disney had all the interviewees in a small auditorium, and we watched a short clip of how Disney is such a fun, magical place for everyone and how you must be positive and enthusiastic all the time, in front of guests, at least. I was offered the job.

In September 2002, I flew to Paris to find out that I was a Disney Village Cleaner, and in that month, the cleaners had to follow approximately ten to fourteen horses – Cowboys and Indians. In between a parade of people with cameras clicking, my job as a cleaner was to sweep up the horse manure for ten minutes every day. My Dad sometimes referred to me as a **"Shit shoveller."** Obviously, they wanted to attract people to go see 'The Wild West Show,' a **Disney Village** Spectacle. By having the parade, they were also attracting people to fork out and spend money.

October 2002 - Here I am in my Disney Village Cleaner uniform with a close Disney-made friend.

During this crazy gap year, I went to the Disney Village a few times after work. I went to the Village Sports Bar a lot, as did most of the working people and the cast members; the discount was groovy. One or two nights in the night club, I saw a load of foam come down from the ceiling. One night I was among the dance floor crazies as the foam poured down onto the dance floor. I couldn't breathe, but managed to get out alive, somehow!

*January 2003- Strangely enough, I met my closest friend at a house party in **'La Residence de la Boiserie'** on a balcony.*

It was only about a four-hundred-metre walk from my apartment. I can remember going to this party, not knowing anyone there, leaving, and then stopping as I neared my own apartment and thinking, "If I don't mingle with people I don't know, then I will always be shy." So, I decided to go back to the party and slowly learned to communicate with people from different nationalities who I had never met before. Then, in a crowded apartment, shoulder-to-shoulder, I edged my way to the balcony. Here I met my best friend, kind of like Romeo and Juliet, except neither of us is gay and no one ended up being poisoned or stabbed! The German chap and I are still friends today. This all happened in my first month in France.

I vaguely recall getting a new roommate, an English chap who had just completed two years at University in England, studying French. I was two years younger and getting paid to work at Disney. I had been there for eight or nine months. I remember my flatmate told me that my level of French was better than his. That seemed crazy to me, as he had paid close to six thousand pounds to learn it, possibly more, and I had lived in France for not even a year and been paid. If you really wish to learn a language, it is financially a lot better to go and work in that country and surround yourself with the language; you'll learn any language easier like this.

I really didn't like my job. My cleaner colleagues all said you must wait at least six months before thinking about changing Disney roles. I thought if I don't ask the lady who employed me in London, I will never know. I went back to Lucy Black to request a change and thought it would be unwise to approach her and moan about how I hated the job, especially as a manure sweeper. So, guess what? I didn't. I just informed my employer that I came to France with a goal in mind; to gain fluency in French, and because of the job, I could not see my goal coming to fruition. She said, "Come back in ten days; if nothing changes, I will hopefully have another job for you by then." I was very fortunate, as Natalie Spearman, the Housekeeping Manager of the big pink four-star hotel, was a French/English lady, and she took a risk employing me, as I was very young and my French was below average.

Since I was still just a teenager, my colleagues often referred to me as the baby in the group. I spent the following eleven months working as a Housekeeping Runner in **L'Hotel Disneyland**. Or for us, **Le DLH**.

By the way, the internet was first used by the public in 1990, and our connection was very slow. It was some 56 K dial-up-procedure where you dialled, waited, waited, and waited. Not exactly like 5-G huh?

*Here in the hotel office, with Raphael, my flatmate,
and in the middle is Mayte, our supervisor. At the
time, pink was not my favourite colour.*

I can recall hearing how many people wanted to work in this hotel. I went from a Disney Village Cleaner to Housekeeping Runner in about a week. Same salary, just very different attire. Shortly before arriving, I had heard that someone was recently fired because they didn't smile enough. Many people in the Disney abode (home) were jealous of me because I did not like my job and was prepared to ask for another one politely. Within the Housekeeping department, I was once voted as Cast Member of the season at one point. I slowly found out that I loved working, and that I am a very hard worker. Please bear in mind that I worked at a massive theme park where there were possibly over a hundred different types of job. It isn't so easy to change jobs inside of such a big organisation. I had also heard about someone being transferred to Epcot, a massive theme park in Walt Disney World, Florida. I suppose I was pretty jealous.

I remember being told often, "Le plus souvent que tu parle en francais, le plus vite que tu vas ameliorer!" "The more often you speak in French, the quicker that you will improve!"

Ten weeks had passed, and I decided to visit Mum and sis just outside of London. First, after leaving 'Chessy Gare' (the Disney station) heading for London, I fell asleep and accidentally got off the train in Ashford, Kent. I thought I had arrived early in London. I guess being tired and confused, I bravely asked someone, "How can I get to London Heathrow Airport?" I remember finally arriving at London Heathrow Airport in a multi-story car park on the second or third level. I called Mum and sis who were in another multi-story car park opposite where I was, and one level down. Fortunately, we found each other, hugged, and Mum drove home to Slough. I do not remember a lot from this visit fourteen years ago, except for my evening meal with Mum.

She had mentioned that Shehrina (sis) was borrowing a lot of money, so I told her not to lend Shehrina any more money as she didn't know how the money was being spent. Actually, neither did I, but I had a feeling she was spending Mum's hard-earned money on that Class A, life-destroying white powder, as I had seen her doing before. Supposedly, it gave you the feeling of incredible strength; it never interested me, though, and to this day, I have not liked the thought of sniffing anything up my nose. Come to think of it; I did shove a little twig up my nose when I was three-years-old, not exactly the same thing, eh? Not sure why I even did that.

Back at Disney, which was now known as Disneyland Resort, Paris, I absolutely loved my year working there. When I first arrived at the Residence de la Boiserie – I hated it. Especially the Belgian couple I had to share the apartment with. To be honest, it was my first time living away from home without the parents; It was quite strange in the beginning. I used to keep lots of my food, such as chocolate, crisps, and drinks, under my bed. While walking out the door to go to work, they (the gay guys) used to raise their middle finger toward me, actually behind my back, I found out later. Not surprisingly, they also hated me. I wanted to change apartments but was told to return to the Boiserie Reception in a month. Once again, I had to wait patiently. To this day, I am not sure what happened, but I got the new job in the Disneyland Hotel, and bizarrely, so did the gay couple I lived with, in the same department, no less. Due to us always being together at work and home, we eventually became terrific friends. I had to get used to seeing two guys kissing daily and would sometimes sit with them and watch something on TV, which was a big box of a TV at the time. Occasionally, I would even have dinner with them.

Reinhard was a Frenchman who worked doing Room Service in the hotel at night. Once, during the year, he had booked a three-week holiday somewhere. I voluntarily raised my hand to say I would cover his shift, not even knowing I would be paid more for working the unsociable hours. I managed to finish the three weeks but did not like it one bit. After one particular night shift, I would usually go straight to bed, but I had a close friend who was leaving, so I walked around Disney Park with her for a while rather than going to my bed. I was to start my next shift at ten pm. I remember counting down the hours I had stayed awake 37, 38, 39 hours ... What made me laugh about this night shift was working alongside this Arabic chef who was often singing songs from his country, obviously in Arabic, so I didn't understand a word. However, I did enjoy listening to it.

I remember coming home with Mum and Lee, her partner, and thinking that the twelve months in Disney had flown by, and it honestly felt like seven or eight months. The expression 'time flies when you are having fun' is so true. I was sad to see it all come to an end. But I suppose you can't stay eighteen forever. As much as I had grown in these amazing twelve months abroad, I still had quite a bit to learn. For example, during my days off at Disney, I used to go to the main Cast Member restaurant backstage and ask for 'Un steak hache, s'il vous plait' – a burger and chips, please. One of my first meals at home in the Boiserie was a pizza. I bought this because I am very careful with my money and while shopping, I saw a box with three pizzas on the label for a shocking 1.50 euro. I thought, *Bargain* until I misread the French instructions and ended up eating small particles of ice in the centre of my cheap pizza. I was hungry, so I ate them anyway. A few months later, I poured the Belgians' thick cream onto my cornflakes, thinking it was milk. In my defence, the cartons did look very similar. I probably immediately brushed that little hiccup off with, "I am sure lots of people have done that."

My Mum had informed me more than a few times that my great grandad, a French chap, was the head chef of 'The Ritz Hotel' in London for more than twenty-five years. Cool, huh? But no, it is not cool because his great-grandson hasn't a clue what to do in the kitchen, apart from making his usual cheese on toast.

April 2003- taken from Notre Dame during Mum's visit

A few months passed in the big pink hotel and I had heard about my favourite band, 'Linkin Park,' performing live in Bercy, Paris. I knew I had to go. Fortunately, a neighbour and a member of the hotel's Concierge team, Georg, wanted to go as well and a colleague did too. I went to buy the three tickets and paid 93 euros, 31 for each. I was handed the tickets, clean, and printed on a shiny card. At eighteen-years-old, I chose to slip them in my inside coat pocket so as not to bend them. This was shortly after my weekly shopping. I got home, and there were no tickets inside my jacket pocket. I nearly cried; they must have fallen out. I decided to repurchase the tickets and this time kept them carefully.

The day came, and the three of us went to the concert in Georg's friend's car. I drank three or four cans of Heineken on route and was a bit dizzy when we arrived. I saw many people walking away from the entrance. Being curious, we kept walking forward, regardless, and saw a sign on the door which read something about getting a refund; due to the 9/11 attacks in New York, they had to cancel and reschedule for the 6th of Sept 2003. I was gutted as I was returning home to England the day before. I thought about it, then chose to get a refund, as the other two were to return to Germany and I had to pay them back.

I thought to myself; I came to France with the goal of gaining fluency in French. There were a few English parties I deliberately chose not to go to, knowing I would speak only English, which would have been a waste of my time. If I wanted to speak English, I would have stayed in England.

As part of the housekeeping team at Disney, we used to go around with these little beeper things attached to our belt. Fortunately, I was at work this one particular day, which meant I was able to meet Elle McPherson, who I knew was a famous supermodel as I used to have a fairly large poster of her on my bedroom wall. Anyway, she requested an adaptor. I brought her an English adaptor, but it didn't work. I had to apologise and get her the American adaptor. She invited me into her room to make sure it worked. I also met Emma Bunton, my favourite Spice Girl (The Spice Girls were a huge English girl band in the 1990s). I met her on Boxing Day (24th of December 2002) and brought her a Disneyland Hotel decorative plate. A few years earlier, Michael

Jackson (a.k.a. The King of Pop) with a rather large entourage visited Disneyland Paris.

One day at work, I had to collect somebody's dirty laundry from the Castle Suite (expensive area) – for the higher-paying guests. I was shocked as I was given a 50-euro tip for two-to-three minutes worth of work. Well, I just stood at the door entrance. I was told these guests were with the Al Maktoum family, a family that is adequately minted.

I still have this crazy Disney memory, when at eighteen, I was walking back to the office. And from out of nowhere came five or six ladies, all dressed head to toe in burkas. I had never heard of a burka, let alone seen one. When they came around the corner, I remember seeing their eyes following me. I'm surprised that I didn't wet my pants!

This was another crazy experience – going to Paris to audition for a job on Disney's entertainment side. We were all supposed to walk like pirates, dance like Mary Poppins, and behave like Mickey Mouse. Then suddenly, we were all split into two groups. Half would stay, and the other half would go home. Fortunately, I was in the half that stayed. But for the last section, we had to copy a dance and then do it for three judges. Although I have always liked dance, I was never very good at it. I suppose I have always had poor balance. Of course, I was sent home following round two, due to not being able to dance.

The Boiserie Reception had a welfare side to it, which arranged interesting trips for its fifteen hundred residents, those who knew about it anyway. I can recall going to a really old vineyard and seeing an old cellar with many bottled wines over seventy-years-old, covered in cobwebs. My close friend, who I met on the balcony, had a friend on the Island of Menorca. I had not heard of this place and may have asked, "Don't you mean Majorca?" In February 2003, my good friend and I went to stay in Menorca for sixteen days with another German friend. Speaking only one word in German, "Guten Tag!" or simply "Hello," made it a little tricky to understand their conversations, but a good lesson in German too, if you wished to learn that language. I didn't but did not mind as we were visiting a new beach every day. This trip cost the flights and ten euros for the petrol I gave to my friend's friend. I'm fairly sure this cemented my so-called 'Travel Bug.'

A fond memory of this Menorcan experience was swimming out to an island approximately half a mile away. I remember doing a dump into the sea and cleaning my backside with seaweed from the sea, another great memory to share with the family later. The swim back was not a lot of fun because as I was nearing the shore, my foot got stuck in a lobster net. Fortunately, my friend was nearby and was able to help me get out of it. Another awkward memory was of an evening we drove to a beach and stopped on the way to buy some San Miguel beer. When we got to the beach, somebody lit a joint and passed it around. Silvio and I lay down on a mat inside what was a kind of mud hut; we were both drunk and possibly high, but we managed to get to sleep without too much fuss. The following morning, we went into the water and lay down facing the shore. Annoyingly, the waves oscillating us on the sand awoke my monster (penis), and suddenly a family in the distance appeared to be heading toward our secluded beach. At this point, I felt embarrassed to get out of the water. I went into deep water and spanked my monkey, as some say, with my head under the water. It took a while as the water was very cold. It happened while floating under the water. Relief!

One of the best night clubs I have visited was on this Island. It was amazingly unreal. At the time, it was just hip-hop music. 'In da club' and 'Gimme the light' were massively popular in 2003. It was called 'Cova d'en Xoroi'; it was so cool, you would walk into a cave built into the rocks, and when getting to the dance floor, there was a massive opening in the rocks, overlooking the sea. I recall this because it was a clear night, and I could see the moon high in the sky, casting a beam of light onto the sea. It was such a good atmosphere.

I thought it strange while at Disney, I met lots of people from all over the world, and one of the prettiest girls, a German girl, worked in the Costume department. Whenever she was at work you would not see her. You would see her as Tigger or Daffy Duck.

You may be wondering, why on earth did I come home, right? Especially after having such an amazing time at Disney. I was not too sure why myself. I was sometimes known as the manager's pet. Perhaps this was due to my strong work ethic at such a young age and my drive to improve my French. I also attended French classes once a week backstage (behind the park) that were arranged by the hotel's manager. I could have stayed; I was liked by all my colleagues and especially the manager.

Nearing the end of my Gap Year at Disney, my Dad made a bet with my stepmom. The bet was that I wouldn't last more than a month, and it was not made directly with me. Just something I heard from Dad the following year. Good to know how little faith he had in his 'once upon a time,' shy son.

A few months before I came to Disneyland, my mother and I attended Reading College to get some feedback on my photographs, another passion of mine. We were fortunate enough to meet the Head of the National Diploma Photography department. It was not a pre-arranged meeting. After meeting the head of the department, he had deferred me for his National Diploma course starting about one year later. As much as part of me wanted to stay at Disney, I decided to go to start the two-year ND course in Photography.

CHAPTER 3: LIFE AFTER DISNEY

On September 8th, 2003 – the first day of the course, I was asked to write my name on the whiteboard in front of everyone. Five years earlier, I had been told by a neurologist that what my symptoms were caused by was a bilateral tremor in my upper arms. As you can imagine, this made me feel more than a little uncomfortable.

Fortuitously, due to the groovy communication skills I had picked up at Disney, I was able to pass the question to some-one else without going overly red with embarrassment. So, my Gap Year from education was not a complete waste of time as I had learned other important life skills, a lot of which cannot be taught in a classroom.

During this two-year National Diploma course, I would commute a twenty-five-minute train journey to Reading Station from Burnham. One of my favourite areas in Photography was shooting portraits.

*April 2004- **Kathy Pang**, a Fashion Student,*
was a wonderful subject to photograph. Because
of this photoshoot, we became friends.

Three or four times a week I would shoot portraits, sometimes with other people from my course. It was a long experience, but I love photography, so it was worth it. I can still vaguely remember the darkroom in Desborough Boys' School, the comprehensive school I attended in Maidenhead. I used to think it was like magic, watching the photo appear on this blank sheet of photographic paper after being dipped into a developer solution, then stop and fix the image. I had never seen anything like it. There was this process that made it seem very magical. The photographic chemicals smelled rancid though, and weirdly, I developed a habit of rushing to the toilet to offload a number two upon entry to the darkroom. Reckon it had something to do with those smelly chemicals.

I made some good friends while taking that course. One woman who comes to mind was Zoe Barker. She started her own photography business on the Isle of Wight. I've been to a few of her exhibitions, once on the Island and twice in London. Every year she sends her own photographed Christmas card, Zoe

Barker. A charming person and a genius behind a camera.

I got along with everyone in the course, but I did mistakenly get involved in a conversation about a photograph with a girl in the course and two of her boyfriends. I tried to offer help but ended up with a warm to hot coffee thrown on my chest. Perhaps I had misunderstood the chit-chat, and the girl had misunderstood my offer to help – a simple misunderstanding?

I met a guy on the course who had the year before been to a kid's camp in the United States. He recommended it, and I liked the sound of it. My classmate and his girlfriend, who was also on the course, went to a Camp America Open Fair in London. It was pretty intense, as we knew when our course was due to finish for the summer holidays so were serious about applying. It was also fun to hear about the different camps and adventurous things there were to do. My friend kept saying, "Ideally, I would like my girlfriend to come," which is something they frowned on, as it looked like they were after a summer holiday to the States. As Camp America was paying for the flights, they arranged everything, the 630 USD salary for the nine weeks seems shocking, but it wasn't too bad. The fee for kids covered food and accommodations as well as classes. I learned that you don't do it for the money; you do it because you love the children. The Camp Open Fair was due to close at 4 P.M., and it was now 3:45 P.M. My friends just stood up from a welcoming booth with big smiles on their faces, obviously because they had been offered a job.

I said, "What about me?" Feeling a bit disappointed, they told me to ask the Camp they had just gotten jobs with. In the last fifteen minutes of the Open Fair after a lot of desperate grovelling, I got the job as a Channel 3 Kids Camp Life Guard. I knew I could swim the breaststroke like a frog, but I still had to go to Edinburgh to get my diving qualification and improve my front crawl stroke (freestyle).

As the summer neared, I struggled to keep my head down and breathe correctly for the front crawl, even though I was practicing a couple of times a week. I was quite pleased when my friend Pete asked me if we could change roles at the Camp. So, I became a Camp Counsellor, and he was a Life Guard with his girlfriend. Result for us both, I avoided doing the Life Guard course in Scotland, and he got to spend the summer tanning (and teaching) with his girlfriend. Channel 3 Kids Camp is a camp for underprivileged kids in Andover, Connecticut. I had an unforgettable experience there and decided to go back the following summer, which I did. This time I went through BUNAC, as they had offered a fifteen-percent discount with Trek America for the Tierra Del Sol trip in Mexico at summer's end. I managed to save over £200, which was very handy. During my time at this camp, it was quite an emotional roller coaster, and for me, a great learning curve. I seemed to bond easily with the kids and became known as one of the better Camp Counsellors.

One of the coolest things the colleagues from camp did was take a large sofa from the camp and bring it to an outdoor cinema. There were about seven or eight of us. Apparently, at the time, there were only about fifty outdoor cinemas left in the States. Typically, what would happen is you would drive your car into a large field and tune in via your car stereo to get audio for the film. Before the film began, I remember a loud sound from the trees nearly surrounding the field. I was told that's the sound of the crickets flapping their wings; apparently, there were loads of them. I do not think the Camp Director knew about this trip. You live and learn, ey!

I remember giving a scolding to a child of eleven because he raised his two fingers to me as he went into the toilets. Later that day, when I told my American cabin mate, Ben, what had happened, he shouted, "Dude, he was just saying that he is going to be two minutes." Well, it wasn't the 'F off' I'd thought it meant. I, of course, felt like a complete doughnut and apologised to the kid the following day.

Basically, after the one-week training course, we would set up camp, which was surprisingly hard in the heat. Our cabins were hot and very stuffy in the woods, being surrounded by trees. It was a wooden hut with no electricity, no glass windows, only four rickety bunk beds, and a small plastic black bin (trash can, I learned from an eleven-year-old in the photographed cabin below). Here, we slept in our sleeping bags for eight weeks. It was me, American Ben, and six children from Hartford, Manchester, Coventry, and Willimantic, among other places in Connecticut. One week, it was just me with seven kids. The wooden hut was known to us as **Cabin B6,** (shown in the next photo).

July 2004- The beds at Channel 3 Kids Camp

I was at Channel 3 Kids Camp in Connecticut between 2004/05 and 2010. The beds have since improved a lot but today it is still an underprivileged Kids Camp and an amazing place for kids and the staff alike. Many of the English staff had spent their summers returning to this Kids Camp and some far more than me. In 2010, I was a Camp Counsellor again, this time during 'Operation Purple Week,' which looked after children whose parents were serving in the U.S. armed forces.

This was the restroom (or bathroom) area on Boys Hill. There was no bath or shower, about eight cubicles behind the wall, and a white garbage bag hung from the wall. The silver cylinder thing has five or six buttons on it. It's a sink.

A normal working day was to wake up the children and get them all dressed, serve them their food at breakfast, lunch, and dinner. Later we check for peed-on sheets. We taught each of the children various things that would help them throughout their lives and took them on campouts where we slept in the woods on a large blue tarp in our sleeping bags, under the stars with the friendly woodland spiders.

It is quite funny reminiscing about that because I used to be terrified of spiders, and I still don't particularly like them. But a young me, nineteen at the time, told the younger kids not to worry about the spiders. We didn't bring enough water on one particular campout, so I volunteered to go back to camp to get more water. On the way back, about twenty metres from camp, listening to children chatting and seeing flashlights, I tripped and fell flat on my face on a root sticking up out of the ground. Fortunately, I fell forward. It was 11 pm, in the woods, and yes, I had a torch (flashlight). When I got to camp, the four litres had become two litres of water. I somehow was able to save two litres of water for the kids despite the fall.

We had to prepare a play (skit) for the first day at camp and play name games with the kids in the evening. After the evening activities, we would tell them a story and get them off to bed. After their story, I would always wait ten-to-fifteen minutes, just to be sure they were all sleeping. Usually, soon after, the snoring commenced.

I learned a few new words by telling a child to put something in the bin and hearing, "Dude, that's a trash can! Wow, you guys call it a bin, that's weird." We also had to fill out forms to speed up the line (queue) waiting to see the Camp Nurse. I asked a kid, "What's your surname?" and wondered why he could not understand. Coming from over my shoulder, I heard, "Oh, I got you, Dude, you should say *last* name."

When we had a weekend off during my first summer, six friends and I decided to share a cabin. Unfortunately, nobody woke up on time to welcome the new batch of kids to Camp, known as new arrivals. I was the last to get dressed, so I sprinted to where I needed to be as soon as I exited the cabin. I didn't see what was about two to three metres outside of the cabin, a thick rope was being used as a wash line about chest/neck height. Needless to say, I *closed-lined* myself pretty good. Fortunately, I was still conscious; I just carried on and got where I needed to be. Spotting the big red rope burn minutes later, a staff member pointed it out.

One day during a break, one of the counsellors read the list of new kid arrivals for the next day and saw that one of them was called Jesus. The counsellor pronounced it "hay-soos", as you would in Hispanic and said, "Cool, we have the son of God coming tomorrow!" I guess he was just being daft.

I fondly recall attending a Drama class at Camp which was full of girls, boys, and staff. A young lad of eleven in my cabin, B6, was by himself. I sat with him and asked what he wanted to do. He said he would like to make up a dance, but no one wants to do it with him. I said, "Don't worry, I'll do it with you." From scratch, we made up a dance to the song called 'Shy Guy,' a Diane King hit in the 1995 film *Bad Boys*. I told him, "I am not a dancer," luckily, neither was he. I had to give up some of my free time, which was not an issue for me, as I wanted this boy to have a great summer break, as he was a great kid. I remember in the actual show, the evening before the kids were due to go home, it was crazy. A-hundred-and-ten kids were screaming his name. I could hear kids in the front screaming, "We love you Ka – rol!!" It was mental. After the dance, the kid was so happy; it made me happy to see his joy.

It was quite surprising to see how easy it was to get the kids' attention, usually by being loud and enthusiastic as though you have something of sheer interest to say. "Who has seen Bad Boys 2?" I asked a group of misbehaving children, who were not listening. But suddenly, they were listening.

A sublime experience, and I was only nineteen-years-old. It was the Tierra Del Sol, Mexican trip. I remember being amazed on the first day at the pre-booked hotel when I went down on the lift (elevator) to get breakfast. It was so different from England. There were lots of guys with long moustaches and an old fella with his huge sombrero (Mexican-style hat) on. We had a very cool tour guide, Sean Martin, who was an amazing guy.

We started in Mexico City where there was a big festival happening. I remember looking up and seeing fireworks blast off the edge of a building and having a boogie with a three-year-old on a raised-up platform in a massive square. We went around the Mexican Peninsula. I remember Palenque for not calculating the right amount of spending money and choosing not to invest in a reasonably cheap mosquito net. That night, I think I must have passed out from being constantly eaten alive by mosquitos. We saw a lot of Mayan ruins, the Chechen Itza (Our guide referred to it as Chicken Pizza) pyramid was very impressive.

This is Chechen Itza. I went up the middle stone stairs and came down on my bum, holding a rope the whole way down.

I found out many years later that this is one of the **New Seven Wonders of the World**. Weirdly enough, when we arrived, we had to wait an hour as we were told that someone had just fallen down the stone steps. Their body was removed, and the leftover blood was just covered up with sand. Lovely!

I got to swim with dolphins in Playa Del Carma and loved it and swam in the Cenotes, which were huge open water wells with many fish in them. I can recall sleeping in a hammock by a **big lagoon** in **Bacalar, Mexico.**

*September 2005- Bacalar, Mexico. Six or seven
of us slept in our hammocks on this pier.*

Mosquito free, it was fantastic. The following morning, the water polo game was fun, and I still don't know the rules. When buying a 330ml glass bottle of Fanta from San Cristobal, it cost 15 pesos. About 15 pence. In San Cristobal, we visited an old church. It was bonkers, adults were walking on their knees cradling their babies, another chap on his hands and knees in front of Coke, Fanta, and 7up bottles all stood up like skittles, and another chap was holding a chicken. The smells inside the church were very unusual, a very old musty smell.

Near the end of this three-week adventurous trek, we all went clubbing in Oaxaca. I met a lovely Mexican girl around my age. We had a boogie, exchanged email addresses, then suddenly I had to leave with the group. I completely forgot about our contact exchange. Fortunately, three or four years later, while tidying my bedroom, I still had the lovely Mexican's email. After that, we became Facebook friends. I recall her inviting me to Madrid, where she studied at the university, but I never went. I should have. Pretty crazy as this was a cute Mexican girl I met on the dance floor clubbing in Oaxaca.

Shortly after my second summer at Kids Camp, a colleague and I went to Washington, D.C. for a few days. We went to Madame Tussauds and a couple of other museums; the Holocaust museum sticks out in my mind. We saw the Capitol building in front of the big lake where Forrest Gump (in the 1994 movie of that name) met Jenny several years before. Just the journey there was exhausting; we had to sleep on the floor of the Airport with all our luggage. Even in our early twenties, we were not overly organised, and hunting for a vacant hotel was tiresome enough due to our lack of sleep.

In the second year at college, I think I only went to classes two to three times a week. It was still a great year. I got to use medium and large format cameras. The college arranged for us to go to Kew Gardens in London, which is a great place to visit if you're fond of gardening or just into nature. In my final year at college, my teacher suggested cruise ship photography, which had never crossed my mind. That night when I went home, using the 56K dial-up (a very slow internet connection), I eventually got to Google and searched cruise ship photography. I called "Muuuum! Do you mind if I call America?"

"What for darling?"

"A job."

"Oh, of course, you can darling, don't be too long!" Everyone of a younger age is called darling in Mum's house.

After searching at the top of the Google list, I found the company headquarters was based in Miami, Florida, in the USA. I was told I would have to fly to Zagreb for the four-day hiring session, which included two interviews. I had not even heard of Zagreb; it's the Capital of Croatia, I found out later. After I thought about this for a while, I figured, "Well, if I do not go, I clearly must not really want the job. If I do go, it will show them how determined I am to get the job." Even though my family said

I would be crazy to go, I went anyway. I really wanted the job and knowing they will have seen how far I had come just for the interview, I felt I was halfway there.

I do remember being in a horseshoe shape of applicants awaiting an interview, and some plum raised his hand and asked, "Can you sleep in the guest cabins?" He mustn't have wanted the job as he was asked to leave the room immediately and did so without a fuss. About five people were asked to welcome the cruise guests to Jamaica, as though we were there in Jamaica. I was scarily one of the five chosen from forty-nine people. I remember just raising my voice and enthusiastically bellowed, "Welcome to Jamaica!!" One of the days there at the hiring session, we were each given five rolls of film (with 24 photos per roll) and told to go out into the city of Zagreb and photograph people and make them interesting and unique. Upon returning, once the films were developed, we had had to choose six of the best photos to take into the interview with us. I remember asking a lovely-looking young couple to touch their ice creams to their noses; hopefully, they could see my attempt at being creative because they did it.

A week before flying out, my photography teacher told me I had about a twenty-percent chance of getting the job. I had a lot going against me, and even the night before the interview in a Zagreb hostel, I was kept awake till around 4 A.M. listening to various European songs by those most likely drunk, people who could not sing and smelling a rather strange odour. Positive thinking and sheer determination got me the job.

"Don't listen to your parents or teachers, do what you want to do, what makes you happy. Most important is to trust yourself!!"

Arnold Schwarzenegger

CHAPTER 4: A NEW LIFESTYLE

At the end of November 2005, I flew out to Miami to start the one-week training session. I can recall being seated in a room and seeing a stocky-looking fellow poke his head out from behind the door, saying: "You must be prepared to give us three to five years of your life to reap any rewards from our company." I was still just a young adult, so this didn't mean anything to me, not sure why I remember this, to be honest. Neither did the next bit; we were each given an A4 sheet of paper informing us of the ship we would be joining to start our cruise ship journeys. Mine read something and then *Jewel of the Seas*, a ship I had never heard of. Upon asking, I found out that it was one of 'Royal Caribbean's' baby ships. It was massive, more than twenty metres longer than the Titanic itself, with fourteen decks. At the time, all this meant nothing to me as I may have only seen one or two TV adverts about Royal Caribbean. We only had four or five TV channels back then, on a big dark grey box of a TV.

I vaguely recall being shown to my room, which was tiny, and introduced to my roommate, an Indian chap, who was very friendly, helpful, and welcoming; also, quite religious. To each their own, he didn't bother me with his religious views. So, we got along great. I noticed a bit of hostility between our team of nine photographers (we called ourselves pho-togs).

In the first week, I was learning everybody's name and always getting lost on the ship. I didn't mind; it was all a new experience. I guess, come to think of it, I quite liked it.

On the fourth day at sea, I ran up some white painted metal stairways to the crew mess (staff restaurant). Running is not allowed on ships, but being so new and innocent, I got away with saying, "I did not know that." I tripped while running up the stairs and had to go to see the ship's nurse, a lovely Canadian lady, uniquely named Crystal. This was in December 2005. We are still friends today via Facebook, even though we live on different sides of the Atlantic Ocean.

Day six came, and we docked in St. Maarten, a Caribbean Island. Since day two, I had been thinking of day six because I knew I would have my first day doing costume; dressing up as a pirate, and getting as many guests as humanly possible to take a picture with me. It was about 7:15 A.M. and fortunately, we were docked next to another large cruise ship, which provided us with a lot of shade. I was awaiting a Croatian girl I went through the training week with in Miami; she was to be the other pirate. Unfortunately, she was followed by three to four officers all neatly dressed in white when she came off the ship. I had no idea what was going on because it was my first day doing this different part of the job. Apparently, she started shouting at her superiors and saying the Sharpie pen used on us for the beard, scars, and other pirate stuff was contaminated and would contaminate the ship's water upon washing it off.

I can also vaguely recall being told to go to a restaurant and get a cork off a wine bottle. I would have questioned what for; we were busy when he asked, and so didn't respond. I did as I was asked and came back with the cork, wondering what it was used for. He lit a lighter and burnt one end of the cork. Then he showed me the burnt end and informed me this is what we use to make a pirate beard. Burnt- cork- end equals Pirate beard. Who knew?

Before I could continue this morning job, I was asked to go to the National Hospital in St Maarten, just to keep this Croatian girl calm in the ambulance, should she have any questions. This situation seemed mental to me as she was a few years older than me and struggled to cope. We were plonked on this ship amid an unhappy atmosphere between photogs and no previous work experience at sea, apart from the one-week training we received in Miami on land. She couldn't cope and freaked out in front of the boss. She was deemed a fruit loop (nutcase) and taken to the hospital to check to see if she was mentally unstable. This way, the ship's Captain had permission to get her off the ship, along with her passport and belongings.

Around this time, the impressive *Jewel of the Seas* docked next to the remarkable *Adventure of the Seas*, both Royal Caribbean cruise ships.

May 2006 - After my morning shoot on the Gangway (walkway leading to the ship).

A photographer from the *Adventure of the Seas* asked me if I would like a ship tour. I was delighted and went on his ship tour. It was similar to the Jewel but a lot bigger; it had an ice rink on board, a huge shopping area, a three-floor auditorium, and a dining room. It seemed like the photographers had to work harder than we did due to its size. I left impressed but kind of glad I worked on the Jewel, the smaller ship.

This was a normal day at sea. You see lifeboats
to the left of the photo.

It seemed a nice itinerary, four months sailing the Carib-bean and then four months in Europe. One early afternoon in Antigua, we had to do a boat drill and stand in the heat for about twenty minutes. Opposite the beautiful scenery on the other side of the ship, you could see dark grey clouds about twenty metres away, and it was starting to rain – a very peculiar event.

On the *Jewel of the Seas*, we had to fill out our hours worked on a small time-sheet. We worked long hours, seven days a week, and we didn't know our next day's work schedule until very late the evening before. I normally wrote down somewhere between seventy-to-seventy-five hours when totalling my weekly hours worked. It wasn't so bad; it was an amazing experience. We were not paid a fixed salary; our salaries were based on commission (though I think that has now changed) and basically, we got a small percentage of everything we sold – cameras, accessories, Cruise DVDs we made and all the photographs we had taken of the guests during their cruise. I recall having to shoot on a private island owned by Royal Caribbean, which was an unforgettable experience. Once, I was offered a chance to work on a Disney Cruise ship. Well, so were a few other people, so it wasn't set in stone. I said I didn't want to change because I knew the *Jewel* was going to Europe in five or six weeks, and I was looking forward to seeing my family, Dad in Dublin and Mum, Lee, and Sis in England.

I remember sailing on a Scandinavian Cruise ship and being nearly Gobsmacked when we went through the Norwegian Fjords. When the ship doors were opened, it made me think of *The Lion, the Witch, and the Wardrobe*, a children's story by C.S Lewis. The six or seven times I went through the Panama Canal was awesome. I would have to wake up early and tend to the camera table sales on that cruise. There was only about a foot gap on either side of the ship as we went through the canal; it was very impressive how the captain and crew made it through such a tiny space.

There was an unusual day where I got to climb a thirty-foot rock wall with a close friend on board while at sea. I lost the race, but it was with a very close friend, so it didn't matter. Sanjay aided me to the top to see the sublime views all around, especially the horizon. This was a cool experience, one that not many crew members get to do since this attraction on the ship was for guests only.

This is me at sea, climbing the rock wall.

I had the chance to climb the well-known Dune River Falls in Jamaica with two very cool onboard guests, Lisa and Malissia, I had just met on that cruise. The ship security rules are stringent, and this was probably not allowed, being seen off-ship, mingling with guests. But it was a memorable experience for me – with two lovely ladies.

During my secondary school days, I was the recipient of quite a bit of bullying; teachers need to clamp down on this. One day at sea, I bumped into quite possibly the most attractive girl on the ship. She said she loved my accent, and she even asked me to repeat the words "Coast Guard." Apparently, she loved the way I said those words. Quite strange, as I had been bullied about my voice three or four years before.

Somewhere near Mexico, I was swimming in the sea, jumping off the back of a small tour boat into the beautiful clear blue sea, fifty yards from an old tribal village. All because some lovely, kind American guest said they would guard my camera equipment, and it was very hot. This was an amazingly short experience, but one I loved and still remember to this day.

It was truly, utterly, a wonderful experience; Mexico's Costa Maya and parasailing with Christine. Not long after I fell asleep at the back of the coach in Mexico when I had become a videographer, I completely missed getting off the coach with the guests due to exhaustion. The guests informed me; after that I didn't miss much. As you can imagine, the seven-day workweek was challenging in the heat. Luckily, I got to see the cliff-diving near Acapulco and a bullfight somewhere in Mexico. This was a very Mexican thing; I came out with a load of children, at least ten, who wanted their photo with me. Perhaps they had mistakenly thought I was a famous actor. I'll never know.

This was a very different, amazing experience. More so was the evening meal, because we were not paying to cruise. Eating the same food that the guests did was so cool. One time, the ship's welfare department organised a back of the ship barbeque for the crew, and our manager, having friends within the Food and Beverage department, permitted us to eat like guests, a burger and fries on the top deck with colleagues during a sea day evening dinner. I remember staring at the moon hanging in the sky like an upside-down floating banana and being amazed by it. Strange but beautiful, I stood staring for close to a minute. I must have looked like someone who had seen a ghost.

A friend from the shops told me a story of a homosexual guy running out of her shop because he had seen a dwarf in the shop. I don't know if he was mentally disturbed or what, but he was serious when he later informed the ship's security people that he feared little people. Then a few weeks ago, on the BBC News App, I read a story about a young woman who is allergic to everything, even her husband. There are sure some crazy things and people in this big world!

Then there were the thirty hours we were stuck in our tiny room due to being sick. My roommate and I were both confined to our room and had to call for room service to eat. I felt terrible, but my roommate seemed fine. But if one is sick, the other may fall sick also, so the ship's policy is to confine them both. Because of this, we were both put into a thirty-hour confinement in our room. Good thing for the ensuite bathroom to do our number ones and twos, tinier than tiny it was. At night, I remember throwing up continuously, wondering if it would ever end. "What could be going on? I hadn't eaten anything."

A few colleagues of mine called me over to look at something from the ship's entrance. I saw an elderly woman walking unbelievably slowly. I can remember thinking, "I hope I am not like that in my old age." I must have been about twenty-two.

When the *Jewel of the Seas* docked in Europe, it was a completely different atmosphere at sea, as the average age for a guest was about sixty-seven, and suddenly our job became quite tedious. "Hi there, would you like your photo taken, lovely lady?"

"At seventy-five-plus, I don't think so!"

So, our salaries went down, partly because the number of photos taken went down. I can recall a time in Europe being likened to the plague and the paparazzi by cruise guests. Not nice comments, but I could understand why we were referred to this way. We also had some training on how to deal with European guests. I thought it was nuts to learn that in Bulgaria for example: whereas when we nod our heads in agreement and shake our heads from side-to-side in disagreement, they do the exact opposite. It came as a shock to me as well. You can get in a lot of trouble with Bulgarians if you don't know that!

As much as it may seem like fun, ship life is certainly not for everyone. I remember being sent back to my cabin to shave on a few occasions and told to go iron my trousers because they looked wrinkled. I hadn't ironed before, but there are some things you have to learn quickly at sea.

I remember being told, "Tomorrow we go to Russia," but we were not allowed to photograph at the end of the gangway as we normally would, due to an issue with Russian customs. That may be different now, though. I was told to dress like a Russian soldier and walk around the ship and get as many photos with guests as I could. It was strange how many people reacted to a uniform. There was a table of about ten Latin Americans who each stood up, one-by-one, to have their photo taken with me as the Russian soldier. I only had to point at them, then point to the ground next to me, without a hint of a smile. This was a tough moment for me, trying not to laugh.

I saw this glamorously stylish girl with a very cool look. I walked up to her and indicated that I wanted a photo with her, using hand movements. She seemed hesitant at first. I very slowly removed her big, bug-eye sunglasses and put them on myself. Then I took my hat off and put it on her head and then pointed at the camera. Fortunately, I had previously learned how to say "thank you" in Russian, "Спасибо! Spasiba."

The ship sailed to St Petersburg, Russia, and docked overnight. I knew most of the crew, especially the concessions, some dancers, casino crew, shoppies (shop assistants), and the spa staff. Our cabins where we lived were all near each other, and we all went to a Russian night club in the evening. At midnight it had an erotic mini-stage show. A bit different from the average club in Europe. When leaving, it was about 3:30 A.M. I expected it to be dark, but it wasn't at all, just overcast and surprisingly bright. I got to browse the Hermitage Museum, which I had never heard much about before, except that it was a famous museum. The Church of the Spilt Blood was an impressive building in St Petersburg. The building looked like it had different coloured ice cream cones on the top, upside-down because of the way the colourful spires were rounded with spikes coming out of the top.

In Europe, for me, one of the most uniquely brilliant places was the medieval town in Tallinn, Estonia, not too far from the ship's dock. It reminded me of the Legend of Zelda, a Nintendo computer game. I had no idea places like that still existed.

A few months earlier in Cozumel, Mexico, I was sitting on a sun lounger, relaxing with my shoppie friends. When we arrived back at the ship, I suddenly realised I had left my compact camera and my wallet under the sun lounger and walked off; silly me! I felt pretty daft, having debit cards in my wallet. When I went back to the sun lounger I was on; it had already been taken.

San Juan, Puerto Rico- a regular stop for the beautiful Jewel of the Seas. A Caribbean island next to an imposing coastal fortress. Castillo San Felipe Del Morro.

An awkward time in the Caribbean for me was walking around the Photo Gallery, aiding guests looking for their photos. When some guests found their photo, they were not pleased because of the pirate in the shot. Luckily, they did not recognise me. I would just apologize and let them know that I would inform the relevant ship agent at the port to change the pirate they use. This happened a few times. Once or twice, they really liked the pirate. Then I would say, "Yeah, it was me!"

Believe it or not, I didn't see any fights at sea, but I did see a few altercations. I was on the upper bunk in this tiny staff bedroom when someone called the room from the crew mess about 3 or 4 A.M., annoying me, as I had to wake up at 5:30 A.M. I think we were due to work on Labadee Island, a private island owned by Royal Caribbean. After work, about 2 P.M., I could sleep till 4 P.M., so I did. We had to prepare for the Captain's Reception at around 5 P.M. As part of our sleeping bunks, there were no barriers, just curtains to pull to make it darker and give us the idea it was nighttime. When my alarm awakened me, I leaned back, assuming there was a barrier there. I must have been disorientated from the early morning phone call the night before. I fell from the top bunk, through the curtains, onto the floor on my back. It was really painful, but I was a man now of twenty-one-years-old, and I was still conscious, so I got up, got dressed, and went where I needed to be. There were no barriers there.

Around this time, I found out through the welfare department onboard that a few of the ship's eight hundred-person crew were going to an Amazing Grace Foundation in Antigua to try and bring some happiness to the lives of eleven young children who had severe disabilities. I jumped at the chance to go with them and share some happiness. Unfortunately, due to work and sailing soon to Europe, I only got to go once. I did, however, get to see why it is called the Amazing Grace Foundation because it was truly an amazing place.

One of the last cruises in the Caribbean on Disembarkation Day, and I was calling guest rooms asking the guests who had things to collect from the Photo Gallery, such as enlargements, copies, prints, etc., before leaving the ship to go home. An elderly American lady just said, "Excuse me, the what gallery?" So, I just repeated what I'd said, and again, she could not understand. This went on three or four times, and I was near tears out of frustration. Then she asked me to "Spell it?" So, I did, "P.H.O.T.O Gallery Ma'am," then suddenly she said, "Oh, you mean the Picture Gallery!" I was nearly crying with laughter because, in my head, that is what I had said.

Just one other thing happened at the ship's training facility in Miami. In a practice session, I referred to a woman guest as Miss. Being that it was an American-owned company, all women had to be referred to as 'Ma'am, and the men referred to as Sir.

I know that I have made the job seem a little glamorous, but remember the long hours worked, and there is no guarantee you'll get along with everyone on the team and that one team irritant could end up being your roommate or a neighbour. Perhaps, if you are a manager of some sort, it would feel quite different. Persistence will get you there.

Interrupting guests at mealtime was part of the job. No cruise ship photographer enjoys approaching a table with a loud voice so that all twelve diners could hear you. To me, it was a rude thing to do, but when speaking to the seniors or the managers about this, you would always hear, "It is part of the job."

It was nearing the end of my first contract at sea – a whole nine and a half months in total. Because I was conversing with an attractive Russian who was selling those Russian dolls outside, I missed the bus to the ship. The next bus had been cancelled, but luckily, I got the last bus out, so I would be back in time to watch the Russian stage production of the Nutcracker Suite with a few of my colleagues, which was fun. I didn't understand a word of it but saw lots of lovely Russian ladies dancing around the stage.

A favourite place of mine was along the Norwegian
Fjords in Norway. It was utterly sublime.

Jumping back a few hours earlier, getting off the bus, queueing, getting through the unhappy-looking customs people, I began to run. I ran as fast as my legs could carry me. Of course, running like that I did not see the two-inch thin nail poking out of the cemented ground. I went flying- but due to the rush of adrenaline running through my body, the concrete fall did not hurt so much. The following day's destination was Tallinn, Estonia, and the first anniversary of my Nanna Rooney's death. I knew I would not be allowed time off to attend the ceremony in Dublin, Ireland. That day, while out and about in Tallinn, I had met colleagues who asked me to go with them. but I just said, "No." I wanted to be alone. I slowly walked back to the shipyard, about four or five minutes from the ship. My head was bowed down. As I looked up, I could recall seeing two large ships docked. I continued walking. I saw the aft (tail end) of the ship that was farthest from me slowly moving back. I thought, "This is very strange." So, I began to walk faster. I was three minutes from the ship; lucky for me, my passport was left with the shipping agent. All I had with me was a box of Das washing up powder. I was in a conundrum as I realised that was my ship sailing away. I waved both arms and shouted, but in the end, I watched her sail toward the horizon. I had mistakenly thought that work started at 6 P.M. which it did, but I had lost track of time and forgot the ship sailed at 5 P.M. I knew about six hundred of the eight hundred staff.

As you can imagine, I was gutted; oh well, life goes on. I waited in a small room with my Das washing up powder while the shipping agent booked me into a hotel for the night. I flew back to London Gatwick Airport the following afternoon and was collected by Mum and Lee (her partner). Mum always finds it amusing as passengers come through arrivals usually with a case in hand. All I had was a small box of Das washing up powder. Fortuitous for me was the shipping agent had left my passport in port. Otherwise, I would have been in a right ole' pickle.

The ship now had two sea days and was going to dock in Harwich, England. I was told to stay in a nearby hotel the night before sailing and then take a taxi to the ship in the morning. When the time arrived, it felt very strange as I had worked on this ship for seven days a week for just over seven months, and I was aware that my first contract was due to end in less than four weeks. I was escorted onto the ship, and everywhere I went on board, it was as though I was a criminal. For me, it was like I had to go to court at sea, that's what I called it, anyway. I had to stand at the end of a long table with the Ship's Captain at the opposite end, five officers, and my manager. I begged for forgiveness and apologised at least three times and tried to inform them as best I could why they should let me stay on board. My manager spoke, though I forget what she said, it was all positive, she did not want me to go. It came down to me not being able to carry out my duties on board in the case of an emergency, and therefore, being irresponsible. I was asked to collect all my belongings and leave the ship. Luckily, I got the chance to say goodbye to my good friend Sanjay Wagela, a Gallery Manager on the ship. I saw a tear roll down his face when saying goodbye. It was an emotional time.

I called to apologise to Image Photo Services and explain what happened. Fortunately, the manager liked me, and the photo cruise concession decided to give me another chance. Although missing the ship is frowned upon, I was given another opportunity, thanks to my manager.

Over this apologetic phone call, I was asked to go to London and get an E1 Medical and then go to Southampton and board the famous *Queen Mary 2*, all in five days to end my first contract at sea. All this happened in five days, after being dismissed from the *Jewel of the Sea*. It was all a bit mental, but I was confident at this point in life, so I did not think too much about it.

All I remember is my time onboard the QM2 was an amazing experience. I met the winners of Strictly Come Dancing. I hadn't heard of them, or of this show at the time, but that was kind of cool. There were many hard times like the hours I worked became longer; the photographic equipment became heavier. But for me, it was just nine weeks. I had a bit of time off during a twelve-day Mediterranean Cruise; I had the chance to go to the Colosseum, into the Vatican, to the Nou Camp - Barcelona's football ground, which at the time was the third-largest football ground in the world with a-hundred-thousand seats. The most memorable day for me was when the ship sailed from Hamburg; there must have been close to a hundred little boats following the Queen Mary 2. People were waving joyously; I watched through a window with a smile. Come to think of it, my last day on the ship was incredible, as I had requested from the Staff Captain if my family could be invited onto the impressive ocean liner and given a guided tour by me and the staff captain had agreed. This was in June 2006; they probably have tighter security nowadays.

August 2006- taken from a deck chair onboard the Queen Mary 2

During the short six-week break, a hurricane hit Miami and pulled down telephone pylons, so I was unable to contact the office. I was quite frustrated at this turn of events. Fortunately, we got in touch eleven weeks later, and my second contract at sea was arranged.

For my second contract, I had to fly from London to Miami, Florida, and stay in a hotel. The following morning, I had to fly to St. Thomas in the Caribbean, then go to the MS Volendam, costing me approximately £1500. It took five or six weeks to make that money back, working seven days a week. So, we had to dip into our own pockets to fly out to the ship we were contracted to work on. The MS Volendam was a great ship; everyone was super friendly. I went parasailing with a colleague, and I was the videographer on tour to an Ostrich farm in Aruba. The good thing was we normally had seven or eight hours off in a day – ample time to relax on the beach.

We were heading back to Fort Lauderdale, Florida, and I got the news that I was to be transferred. My reaction was, "You must be joking!" I had to fly to Frankfurt, Germany, and then wait three or four hours before transiting to Osaka, Japan. I checked a world map and saw I was travelling the long way around the world; it must have been cheaper that way. I did not pay for it and was still a young adult at twenty-three, so the forty-eight-hour journey was nothing. I was to join the MS Statendam, another Holland America cruise ship. A few weeks into the cruise, I was told we were going to cross the International Dateline, so there will be two May 11ths. Actually, to this day, I'm still not sure how that happens. But it wasn't for me to know why, so I just got on with it.

By this stage, I received a promotion and was now a Senior Photographer, and I was also trained in videography. I can recall sailing to Alaska and going on the guest tour in Dutch Harbour. It was -twenty-or-thirty-degrees Celsius, and all I had were summer clothes as I had previously transferred from the MS Volendam in the Caribbean. To add insult to injury Lufthansa lost my luggage and which included 3000 USD that was in the missing suitcase. I borrowed coats and jumpers from colleagues or neighbours as I was told to expect the worst. That day it was painfully cold, bizarrely, in almost every shop, there were Filipinos who had set up business there. I say 'Bizarrely' because I had colleagues from the Philippines and knew it was mostly a hot place. They said the pay was much better in Alaska, and you get used to the cold weather. Fortunately, my caring mother was on the case, and she got in touch with Lufthansa in Osaka, Japan, where the suitcase went missing. I still had to live on a cruise ship for ten days waiting for my luggage. Thanks to my Mum, the money was still there when it arrived at a port in China ten days later.

While shooting a run around the outer top deck that would benefit cancer research, a female runner after the run showed a lot of hostility toward me because I did not photograph her. It was impossible to take her photograph; she always ran behind her friends. I did feel very bad about not having taken this lady's photo, but there wasn't much I could do for her but sincerely apologise and inform the manager.

Anurag Gaur, the manager, was a lovely Indian man with a strong Indian accent who used to, upon request, sometimes sing the Indian song 'Chaiyya, Chaiyya' for me in the office/laboratory. I had first heard this song in an American film called 'Inside Man.' The lady was offered free photographs and an apology from the manager, and she left the Gallery happy enough.

Just before setting off to Alaska, we did a month of sailing around Asia. I vaguely remember how beautiful one city seemed to be. I recall walking down Zhong Shan Lu (Road) in Xiamen and being amazed at its uniqueness. Zhong Shan is the name of a great person in China. Almost every city in China has a Zhong Shan road or park.

One bitterly cold day in Dutch Harbour, while walking back to the ship, which was in sight about half a mile away, I was stopped by a four-by-four about twenty metres in front of me. There was a light blizzard around me. A guy got out of his car and started shouting at me, fortunately due to the blizzard and windiness, he shouted so I could hear him. I had not realised I was about to walk across a runway, and there was a small aircraft due to land. I don't know who he was, but that man probably saved my life.

Another time, I can recall being at Glacier Bay on an Alaskan Cruise and seeing large chunks of ice falling into the water from a big block of ice. Apparently, it is known as 'White Thunder' because of the loud thunderous sound that comes with the ice breaking off.

There were some good times on Holland America ships, we were allowed to eat with the guests, and the food was very nice, best strawberries I have ever tasted (from Dominica, I think). I was to go on a guest whale-watching tour when I saw a boat, packed with Americans, that erupted in ebullience when they saw the black back of a killer whale; it didn't even jump. I was unimpressed, and after all, I was just doing a job, videoing the guests. Next, I went on an Eagle Spotting tour in a raft-like boat with this chap in the middle rowing. When asking that question, I would never ask; his answer was, "Yeah, strong like bull!" That was an interesting excursion. It was somewhere around this area I saw snow at sea. At the time, my manager, with ten years of experience at sea, said this was the first time he had seen snow at sea. How lucky was I?

Close to the end of my second contract at sea, at twenty-three years old, I decided to write my letter of resignation. Even though I spoke English to my current business manager, he said, "Because you are fluent in English, you may get ahead quicker than other nationalities." He reckoned that within two years, I might become a Business Manager. I enjoyed being a professional photographer but did not wish to get stuck in the cruise ship lifestyle. So, I decided to leave at the end of my second contract.

CHAPTER 5: LIFE AFTER THE SHIPS

Within a week of being back at home, I had booked an African Adventure trip with the tour company Acacia Africa. I had unexpectedly spoken to a manager from this company who persuaded me to do the full fifty-eight days – Nairobi, Kenya to Cape Town, South Africa. It was quite a challenge, as ninety-five-percent of this trip was camping and some in the bush. We moved from A to B in a large overland truck, not a bus! We often ate by the roadside, washed our dirty dishes, and then got back on the road again. This trip was utterly amazing, from visiting the spice Island of Zanzibar to coming near face-to face-with a mountain gorilla, braving a lion encounter, sky diving twice in one long weekend to seeing the longest waterfall in the world in Zambia, the *Victoria Falls*. It was an epic adventure holiday.

The first two weeks were in Uganda, and trekking to see mountain gorillas was the most physically challenging thing we did. It was about an hour and a half trek to get to the gorilla site, and I was the one person who didn't receive a hiking stick because there were none left. I still remember when our small group arrived seven metres from a family of twelve gorillas; my hands were not very steady. Fortunately, the lovely lady in front agreed to allow me to use the top of her head as a tripod. I can remember someone in our group asking, "How many gorillas are left in Africa?" He was told about seven-hundred-and-fifty, and that was in 2007. I found that very sad.

The black blob on the left of the next image is actually a gorilla. This is where the focus should have been. Instead, I captured a nice piece of greenery.

June 2007- Taken with unsteady hands in the Ugandan mountains.

This was a life highlight for me. Having the chance to go into the gorilla's natural habitat for an hour was amazing. We just sat there and watched; I had the feeling they knew we were there, though.

We stopped at a very cool camping site. It was pouring rain when we arrived and sorted out our sleeping arrangements, which usually involved pitching the tent. I went to chill out near a bar. It was a dimly lit room with a high cascading, beautifully lit indoor waterfall. This was very strange, being almost out in the middle of nowhere in Uganda. Many of the roads we travelled along were dirt tracks and very bumpy. Our two tour guides had been on the road for a year and a half, so they were quite experienced. We had the chance to see the Pygmy people, which was a great experience to see how they lived and survived. Pygmies are very little people who live up in the mountains in Uganda. Their homes were made of mud and straw. It was a five- or six-hour journey in a small white van then twenty to thirty minutes on foot, and finally at least a half-hour boat trip to get there across Lake Bunyonyi. For me and others in our group, it was unfortunate to see these people and learn about how they survived. What amazed me was how happy they all seemed with no or very little possessions. Not one of the seventy or eighty that were there had shoes or socks, and the nearest shop was a minimum of a hundred miles away. I cut the sole of my foot in the small white van. Australian Ben, the driver, just said, "Stuff it with dirt, you'll be all right!"

We got some rest at a nice campsite in Jinja, with a cool open outside bar, about fifty metres from the roaring River Nile. I still remember one night at this campsite, Ben, the truck driver, and the group encouraged me to play a drinking game. Rather cleverly, everyone went to bed, and instead, I went down some steps built into a grassy hill and went to an outdoor, bricked up, roofless shower next to the River Nile. It was here that I lost my virginity. I was very drunk.

Maasai Mara National Game Reserve

We passed back through Kenya and went to the world-famous Maasai Mara National Game Reserve. Because I was in extreme pain "downstairs, the tour guides decided to take me to Kenya's National Hospital. We had to wait a while; the doctor's probably thought, "Oh, not another stupid young foreigner." They gave me some knob cream, and we went on our way. According to Ben, I had "forgotten to preheat the oven, and had put the bun in dry."

I had the chance to see the Maasai men at home in their village and was given a tour. I recall being told a story of the guide's five wives. Crazy huh? I asked, "Do you have a favourite wife, then?" That was definitely a juvenile question but luckily, he laughed.

And then on to Tanzania, where we went through the amazing **Serengeti National Park**.

The Serengeti National Park.

Here, you could see grasslands for miles and even see the horizon, and oddly enough, there was one solitary tree, definitely something new; I had not seen this before.

Here we all boarded a reasonably large boat. The journey was four or five hours, the sea was rough, and many people from our group were seasick. We finally got to Zanzibar Island and pitched our tents on the sand; we stayed four nights and five days. This was super cool as we set up our tents facing the sea. I found out from a local guide that Freddie Mercury (the lead singer of Queen) was born here. I can remember going to a cinnamon plantation and buying lots of Ylang Ylang foot cream, made from the inland spices for the family and meeting Lisa, who I met on a cruise ship about nine months before.

The next stop was Malawi. This was an interesting stop where I bought two large curios (woodcarvings), each about fifty-to-sixty metres long, from an outdoor shopping market on the roadside. I paid fifty USD for the two curios. Back home, they would have been more than one hundred pounds. I gave them to Mum and sis as gifts, but they returned them both years later.

Along the same road minutes before, the tour guide thought it would be funny to speed up into a black cloud on the road. He knew what the strange-looking cloud was; we did not. As it was a bright summer's day, we had two or three of the truck windows wide open. When the truck hit this dark cloud in the road, panic ensued among all the truck passengers. The dark cloud turned out to be millions of tiny flying insects. It was a horrible feeling as many of the insects flew into the truck. We all panicked in our own way; I immediately covered my face with the book I was reading. The truck driver pulled over shortly after, seeing everyone was in panic mode and told us how hilarious it was to see everyone this way.

August 2007- we camped at Kande Beach, right
next to Malawi Lake, for three nights.

Here, in these waters, I attempted a PADI course to learn
how to scuba dive. I failed as I struggled to clear the mask.
I wasn't bothered and I went snorkelling instead. It is just as
much fun.

Then we went down to The Waterfront campsite in Liv-
ingstone, Zambia. The site was only a short drive from **Victoria
Falls,** which was sublime. A lovely day. That's mist you see in the
photo.

August 2007- Victoria Falls

Victoria Falls is the longest, and possibly the highest, waterfall in the world. I recall crossing a wooden footbridge, and while looking toward the Gorge, I saw a massive rainbow which formed a circle in the spray from the waterfall. It was mesmerising. I went up in a micro-lite, which is an outdoor aircraft, to view Victoria Falls from the air. It was only for fifteen minutes, but I loved every minute of it. A day or two later, we went to the Gorge, and I tried the Gorge Swing and the Superman Jump over the gorge, pretty 'poop your pants stuff,' but at the young age of twenty-three, you'll try anything. A day or two after I went on an Elephant Trail on Ellie, the elephant. I did this with a local guide, and no, he hadn't heard of Nellie the elephant.

The next day I wanted to do the **Lion Encounter,** which was very cool, but a bit scary, especially when they rolled onto their backs, and the tour guide asked me to crouch down next to them for a photo. I did so without a fuss, but then he said you must put your hand onto one of them, just for the photo. As hesitant as I was, I knew there was a man with a tranquilliser dart gun very nearby, and humans had raised these two tame female lions in Zimbabwe from a young age.

August 2007- The Lion Encounter

Toward the end of my walk with the lions, we were supposed to see lion cubs. Due to an elephant just passing by, the cubs were scared away. So, it didn't happen.

All the cool things that I have mentioned above were optional extras for which the guests could pay. My wonderful memory with the lions has now been framed and placed on the bathroom wall, opposite the toilet. I did not put it there.

August 2007- after about a week or more in Zambia, we drove further down into Botswana. I saw the bush families in Ghazni.

Here I first heard of their local language, the Click language, also known as Xhosa, which is filled by constant clicking sounds. It was strange listening to them communicate. We visited their village and saw how they make fire and find water. They had what looked like a loincloth around them, and that was it; the rest of their bodies were naked. Next, we drove on to see the Ngorongoro Crater, at the conservation area; it was just a massive hole in the ground, but gigantic. I think it was formed by a meteorite hitting the Earth thousands of years ago, possibly millions of years ago.

I remember it got very cold here at night. Our driver, Ben, and I shared a tent. A knocking sound came from the side of the tent that had awakened me. Ben told me to be quiet and go to sleep, as according to him, it was a rhino. Gullible me was terrified. A knock, knock sound came again and again. Around 3 A.M., the fly, or waterproof tent cover became detached, so we had to get out of the tent in the pitch black, couldn't find our torches, to reattach the fly. I was terrified, so Ben told me it was the wind causing the fly to bang against the tent, causing the knocking sound. It was tricky in the darkness but in the end, we got there. He had nicknamed me Handbag, and I jokingly called him Bungalow because he had little intelligence upstairs. I think we woke up most of the twenty-four in the group. Thankfully they could find their torches, so we ended up having a little light.

At the same place the following morning, we loaded the truck as we were all ready to go onto our next destination. We all needed to shower before we went. Going into the shower, I heard it was very cold; I may have thought, "I'm a man; I can take the cold." When I got into the outdoor shower facility, there was a queue for each shower. Hearing the screams coming from big, strong, muscular men scared me a little. Skinny me didn't scream. I just had my lips pressed tightly together and showered very quickly.

Next was one of my highlights of the whole trip; we went to the **Okavango Delta in Botswana**.

August 2007- this is a photo of the very large swampy inland Delta, the largest in the world.

We got to a place within the Delta where we could pitch our tents. We travelled via mokoros (tiny wooden rafts). That evening, the locals made a large fire, and we played their camp games around the fire; it was a lot of fun. The following morning, we went for a morning swim in the Delta which also was great fun.

On to Namibia, we drove further south through a desert, it seemed, until we came to a stop at a high sand dune, Dune 45, I believe. We had been told that it was around three-hundred metres in height, and we could walk up to the top. I walked about halfway up and could feel and see it was getting windy. So, I decided to come back down, which turned out well as I was the first to eat the warm porridge. I became very friendly with the two guides who had asked me to delay my flight back home. Of course, I tried to but would have ended up having to stay another two weeks at the cost of more than three hundred pounds just for flights. I was pretty exhausted from all of the travel, so in the end, I decided against it.

Dune 45, Namibia – around 300m high.

Next, we ventured down to Swakopmund, Namibia, a coastal city. It was amazing, as here we had the chance to go skydiving. I was definitely up for this; this said while still on the ground! I did not want a five to ten-minute DVD for 40 USD. After the jump, when watching everyone else's DVD, I thought to myself, "I want one of them." Fortunately, there was still time, so I recall paying another 250 USD for another skydive two days later, but this time I got the DVD for free. Bargain! Not really, as I could have saved a lot more, but it was cool this time because it was just the guides and me, in a sea-green open-top VW Beetle. We went for a drive around the small airport. It was crazy cool in the open-top Beetle. A few days later, the day before it was time to leave Namibia and head to Cape Town, we all (about twenty-four of us) went to this club/bar for a boogie or just a drink. I had stopped drinking at the age of twenty-one as my father's a binge alcoholic. I did not want to follow in his footsteps, and an Uncle had said to me it would be wise if I drank less. I was never a big drinker, not even of water, so it was easy enough to stop altogether for me. A bar dance was about to take place, and the guides wanted me to participate. I'm not a dancer, but I have a few cool moves from the end of the movie 'Hitch' and what I've picked up online. I was the only sober guy doing it, so, surprise, surprise! I won a bottle of most likely their cheapest wine for our group.

Swakopmund, August 2007- following the skydive

In the last week, we stopped at Fish River Canyon, the second largest canyon in the world after the Grand Canyon. It was amazing, a sight to see. When we finally arrived in Cape Town, we went to a famous restaurant, visited a township there, and saw Table Mountain from a distance. That was it; I had a pre-booked flight home to London Heathrow Airport the following day.

Ben and I had a bet to see who would either shave or get a haircut first. It was a draw because we both lasted the full length of the trip. By the trip's end, I felt well-travelled and looked like a Yeti.

Even though I had asked the group, who had informed me that you're allowed two check-in bags, little did I know I had to pay 120 pounds in South Africa to get the large wood carving on the flight from Cape Town to London Heathrow. Fortunately, I had the money on me.

It was strange coming home from this two-month adventurous journey. I felt like I was now in a bubble watching kids crying because their parents had said, "No!" and couples arguing, most likely over the littlest thing; this wasn't so common in Africa. It was one of my best experiences ever, and I hope to return one day. "Hey, Heini, what does TIA stand for?" "This Is Africa."

The Australian truck driver wanted to enter a staff photographic competition, something like that, anyway. He went through the photographs on my camera and transferred three or four to his camera since he knew I used to be a cruise ship photographer. I never found out if he won that competition but that made no difference to me anyway. I know that three of my photos were selected for the Acacia – Africa's annual travel brochure, and I appeared in two of them.

August 2007 - a photo of Ben and Heini, two tour guides, and me, in the middle of Namibia during the fifty-six days on my adventurous African trip.

CHAPTER 6: BRING ON THE NEXT EXPERIENCE

It was September 2007, and my goal was to find a place in Thailand where I could teach. Only one slight problem, I do not hold a degree. I did not want to go there and teach illegally and possibly risk deportation. I had to get hold of a teaching certificate, which I did. I did a one-month intensive course in Stanton School, London; the third week in, I was falling asleep in class. It was a really enjoyable course; I met some lovely people in that course, who gently woke me up. I had never heard of this franchise EF (English First), but I applied to them anyway. Little did I know they would contact me and request I teach in the South of China, close to Thailand. In their Shanghai Head Office, an English manager persuaded me to teach in the South in Guangdong, to be precise.

I was given a choice of four EF schools to work at. I chose Huizhou City after seeing some impressive scenic photos. A couple of weeks later, I was there. I arrived on a bus, and it looked nothing like what I had previously seen in the photos they had sent to me, although this did not cross my mind. It was one of the least homely-looking places I had ever seen.

A few days before, I stayed with a second cousin in Hong Kong and went to see this massive golden metal Buddha on a hill. It was awe-inspiring. It was overcast, and I was alone, so I didn't take too many photos. I remember the long cable car journey. I was alone in the cable car; it was very windy, and there was a window wide open on the opposite side of the car. Nearly pooped my pants with fear that the car might blow off the cable. I could hear a loud whistling sound blowing through the open window.

On my first day, I remember meeting Apple, one of the Chinese staff, who was eating an apple with her mouth wide open while she spoke when I first saw her. She was munching away on this apple. I could see how different most of China was from the Western world. For starters, there appeared to be no manners. In the foreigner's staff room, through a window, you were often listening to guys hacking up phlegm and spitting it out. It sounded disgusting. Unfortunately, we just had to ignore this horrible sound.

One of the first things I noticed when I began working as an English teacher was the locals would often ask you, "Ni chi guo le ma?" or "你吃过了吗？" which means, "Have you eaten yet?" Just like the English ask, "How are you?" or "Alright, mate?" I used to think it was none of their business if I have or haven't eaten but I guess, in China, I learned to become more tolerant of other people because their ways are different.

The first apartment I shared was with a Filipino and an older South African chap who were both very nice. The apartment was paid for by the EF school. One of the young Canadians there, also in his mid-twenties, had spotted me. He lived like a pig, but he always blamed the mess on his two roommates whenever I was there. I was young and naïve, he always invited me out, and I didn't pay for a single thing in the six weeks following my arrival. There was a new building just built, and he wanted to be at the top but needed a roommate to share the cost. I was an easy target, and I did not realise how much he seemed to dislike his roommates. On the last day, he cut his nails, toenails included, and left the clippings under his bed. What a minger!

My second apartment was directly above a large shopping centre and a giant Walmart. Also, there was a basketball court and a pool on the roof, which we never got to see as they were still building. A nice, brand new building with a nice big balcony, and we lived on the **25th Floor**.

To us, it became known as The Walmart Building.

EF school sent a few of us to Nantan, a local primary school. One time in the summer, I went to the drinking fountain as I had done many times before in my primary school eighteen years earlier. Only in the South of China, the drinking fountain water was very, very warm.

Some students attended the EF school, and at the end of their course, the parents came to observe a class and ask any questions relevant to their child. They could ask me about the course at any time, though.

The children lived locally. I had no more than fifteen in a class. I remember a student telling me about her day and how she had told me that at school she had sixty students in her English class and only one Chinese teacher. "That's a lot, isn't it?"

*Here are some of my Nantan children in their playtime
away from their classrooms.*

My bedroom was tiny, and I ended up living out of a suitcase for two months, which I got used to. In contrast, this Canadian chap had a massive bedroom and two large cupboards. He turned out to be not the honest guy I'd once thought he was. I should have put my foot down in the beginning and insisted I have one of his cupboards. Unfortunately, even at twenty-three, I was young, naïve, and a bit of a pushover.

The apartment was a twenty-minute walk from EF Huizhou, an English Language Institute. In the summer months, I would walk to school in a T-shirt and, ten minutes into the walk, it would randomly start pouring. This occurred quite a few times. I didn't like this at all, but it was something you had to get used to. Sometimes, there would be a row of seven or eight prostitutes who would occasionally pull your arm on the walk home in the evening. My Canadian roommate showed me some of the back streets. I was pretty surprised when we passed seven-to-eight pink shops. Inside each shop were about twenty youngish ladies dressed in long white silk dresses who would sometimes say, "Massa-geee!" in a high-pitched voice. Word of mouth said that included a happy ending, but I never went into one of the pink shops to find out.

During my time in China, I, unfortunately, saw a large piece of meat hanging from a grocery store hook. When I asked what it was, hearing the word "dog" really made me feel sad. Apparently, it's only in the South of China, Guangdong area, where they eat what most people call pets.

In my third and final apartment, I figured I should browse the local shops. I walked into a tea shop and saw eight or nine elderly men in a circle, all drinking tea. They asked me to sit down, but I immediately refused. Three or four of them insisted, so I sat and had a cup of cha (cha being Mandarin for tea) with them, from a cup that looked to be the size of a shot glass. A cool experience.

I was once on the way home from work, and I was dragged into a group of elderly women, all practicing Tai Chi, a martial art that was taught as an exercise that was good for your balance. I had awakened, to spend a penny (go toilet) a few times to see over my balcony, elderly women practicing Tai Chi outside at seven o'clock in the morning. I went back to bed.

I remember hearing this very loud, extraordinary sound all the way up in the apartment. We had a relatively large balcony that we ran to, trying to figure out what this unusual sound was. The following day in school, we asked the Chinese staff, curious to know about the sound the previous evening. It was every car, lorry, and motorbike on the road beeping their horns in mourning for those who died in the 2008 Sichuan earthquake. The whole thing had lasted for just a minute or two.

Yet another strange day in China, this time when I was

walking out of my apartment, I suddenly found I was walking among huge, very realistically sculpted dinosaurs which were a lot bigger than I was. I saw these huge dinosaurs the following day, erected in the shopping mall just under my apartment. They became quite a photographic attraction.

Stranger still, how about walking along and seeing a small child squatting with a massive lump of pooh hanging from his bum, hovering over a newspaper? Mum was bent over watching her child. I immediately stopped in shock, crossed the road, and then left the ugly sight behind me.

Having the tiresome job of working in a kindergarten was pretty much like babysitting for these kids, as the majority knew very little English. It was only for two hours a day, and we knew nothing about these kids.

One evening, a close friend and I went to a nearby park; we had just bought two red lanterns about forty-five-minutes prior. It was amazing watching the lanterns fly off into the sky. On another occasion with this same friend, we went kite flying in the same park. There were about fifty-to-sixty or more kites in the sky when looking up to the clouds. When it was my turn, I was terrible at kite flying. I suppose it was my first time. Just after that, on the way to play badminton, we bumped into some of my friend's old school buddies. We stayed with them and played hacky- sack with a small beanbag-shaped ball instead.

I recall having to teach three- and four-year-olds. I had a mini beard. The kids entered the class, and seven out of nine started crying and shouting, "Wo yao Mama!" "I want Mummy!" Not really surprising; I was politely told by 'Lucy' the Chinese boss, that it would be wise to shave my beard. Of course, I did.

There was a lovely young lady at this kindergarten where I worked who was like a translator for the foreign staff, I only attended for two hours a week, so I had limited knowledge of the kids. In quite a few of the classes, it felt like we were babysitting the children. She was great with children and had a great personality when interacting with the staff; she was single and spoke English. I randomly bumped into her outside a shopping centre about five months later. To my surprise, she was getting married and planning her wedding in a few months. I have heard from colleagues that people there expect you to be married in your young adulthood if you're a woman. To me, that seems more than a bit unfair.

I can recall a day after work when leaving the building, this man, looking a little lost, came into the building. I offered help; he told me that he was going to be a student with EF. Upon asking his name, he replied, "My name is Book," and I thought for a moment then replied. "Hi, nice to meet you; I am one of the EF foreign staff," trying to put his mind at ease. I then walked him to the lifts, went to the Fifth Floor with him, and introduced him to the Chinese staff, who could get him registered.

I can remember another time, waiting outside a local primary school where there was no taxi. It was suggested by the school that I walk towards the EF school and try to hail a taxi. Randomly, a police car stopped and said, "Where are you going?" They were going in the same direction as me, so they said I could ride with them. Now that is a strange feeling, riding in the back of a police car when you haven't committed a crime!

I was invited on a weekend trip to Guilin with a friend from the EF school. It was a twenty-two hour bus trip there and back, which was very uncomfortable as we drove in an old Chinese bus, forty-odd Chinese, and me.

March 2009- the mountain range in Guilin is stunning and unique. It was used for the creation of the mountains in James Cameron's film "Avatar".

Wow, I didn't realise I was so tall!

We stopped for lunch during the 1 hour boat trip on the Li Jiang river in Guilin.

In the fifteen months I spent there, I never saw a Chinese girl smoking in public. Actually, at that time, I maybe saw one or two birds flying in the sky due to Chairman Mao killing all the birds, claiming they carried deadly diseases. It was rare to see a blue sky; normally, it was cloudy, possibly caused by pollution.

I met an English friend, Barnaby, in Xiamen, which was a

nine-hour bus trip. This city is probably in my top ten favourite cities. It is, without a doubt, a must-see. Barnaby was a friend from the CELTA course. He studied Mandarin at Xiamen University and studied Tai Chi, and taught Philosophy to small groups of Chinese. I was lucky enough to sit in and watch one of his philosophy classes, which was a learning curve for me, too.

During this visit to see my friend Barnaby

Some of the food was not nice at all. Especially the spiky fruit that smelt of pooh, called Durian. I very nearly vomited when I had the Durian flavour pancake. In this restaurant, hearing the translation of some of the food was almost funny. "This is the cow's intestines, and this is pig's testicles!" I shan't be having any of that then.

I went to dinner with this beautiful ex-student, having been invited out to a restaurant. I noticed a small pile of chicken bones built up beside her plate, where she had spat them out. After the meal, she wasn't as beautiful to me as she once was.

I obviously became fed up with being treated like a mug. Once again, I moved to another apartment, and again, it was a new building. It was a bit too spacious for one person, but it was very cool in that it had a large outdoor balcony and was over-looking a river.

Daily, I would walk through a very narrow shopping centre to work. I thought it quite amusing, the **big-eyed mannequins**, perhaps trying to look like the tall Western ladies.

April 2009- the mannequins were so, amusing,
I decided to photograph them.

Once I went to the cinema to see a Chinese film with subtitles in Mandarin, it was a bit weird to see 'Mei Lang Fan' and only understand "Wo ai ni" which means, "I love you." I remember seeing *Mission Impossible 2* near Paris when I was on a French Language Exchange at the young age of sixteen. Then again, I understood one word, "Magique!" which, interestingly enough, sounds a lot like the English word "Magic!"

On another unusual day reading by the river, I saw a pretty Chinese girl out running. I asked, "Qing wen, ni ke yi bang wo ma?" "Excuse me, can you help me?" She sat next to me and began offering help. When we stood up to go home, it turned out she lived in the same apartment building as me just one floor higher up. I hadn't seen her before this day. There were loads of apartments she could have lived in. Strange, huh?

I can recall going to a crowded swimming pool with a female friend and people asking, is this your husband? I suppose I was the only foreigner. They must have thought that I was a monkey half-breed of some kind because in general, most Asian's have very little body hair.

My final memory was packing my years' belongings and giving my bed cover, sheets, and pillows to a homeless guy just outside of the building. We didn't understand each other, so I gave them to him, saw his face light up, and walked away. No words were needed!

The day before I was to leave China, the senior teacher's wife was a hotel manager, so she could get me a stay in the 5-star Kande Hotel with a forty-percent discount. There was a steam room in the room, which added a unique touch. I walked down a corridor and came across about thirty Chinese girls, all dressed in pink and blue tight-fitted dresses with backs against the walls either side of the corridor. They just kept on saying, "Ni hao!" or something like that. It was a unique experience.

I arrived at the international airport in Hong Kong and was

told I needed to pay 230 USD for excess luggage. I was very hungry, without money, as I'd forgotten the password to my credit card, but for a few coins, and Mum kept calling. I was running around the airport with a Nokia 3210 pressed to my ear, Mum kept banging on about tweeting someone, which frustrated me a little, as I had no idea what she was talking about.

Fifty minutes or less before they called for boarding, I saw the flight cabin crew and pilots getting onto the plane. I spoke to one of the pilots. "Excuse me, sir, please tell that lovely lady at the check-in desk to put me on the flight, just say I am your nephew or something like that." He could see my desperation, and fortunately for me, the pilot managed to cancel out the 230 USD. And luckily, on the back of the boarding pass was a free plain burger from McDonald's with a purchase. I had a few coins on me but was still five or ten cents short to buy McDonald's cheapest thing. Somebody was good to me that day, and a lovely lady gave me the small fries and free plain burger, which filled me up while I waited for the flight. Not at all a McDonald's type of eater, but that day, that free plain burger tasted delicious.

Approximately a twelve-hour flight later, from Hong Kong to London, and I was home.

It was June 2009, when I was twenty-five that I realised had no real plan, just to learn to drive and then do some volunteering. A local woman who was going to find me some volunteer work must have changed her email address, or she was super busy and did not reply to my emails. I soon became very bored. England was in a recession, and it wasn't easy job-hunting, and it also took me eleven months to pass my driving test. For some reason, I decided to weigh myself, and I saw I had lost at least ten kilos in China. I did hear when I was there that all foreigners in China lose weight. I gained twelve kilos back just from Mum's home-cooking in the next four months. I kept taking the Chinese Mandarin lessons, even after my return home.

CHAPTER 7: WHAT NEXT?

I started to think that I might be going crazy, every day seemed long, boring, and the same. I was restless because I had travelled a lot in my early twenties, I had no friends in the new place we had recently moved to. I would spend my days talking to myself or my black cat, Willow. I had an Uncle telling me to apply for similar jobs in Vietnam. Mum was telling me to apply for Job Seekers Allowance, another Uncle telling me "there are jobs out there," and Dad telling me, "Ah sure, you know we all love you; you have done more travelling than the entire family." Silly me, I began thinking and saying that my balance is worsening. In the end, I signed up for the dole (JSA) and kept looking for a job.

Ah-ha, I had an idea. As I live very close to the local football team's football pitch, I thought I'd pop over to see their manager and inform him of my youth as an excellent goalkeeper. I guess I hoped I'd be given a trial. Again, my close family tried to put me off, but I went to ask anyway. Actually, glad he wasn't there. My family was right; it wasn't the job for me.

After a match, when all the lads would go to celebrate in the pub, I'd more than likely go home. Going drinking in a pub, then running to the toilet an hour later seemed a bit of a waste of time, money, and energy to me!

I never liked going to the job centre. It would usually take fifty minutes to get there by foot and train. Most of the time, I would sit patiently waiting for two or three minutes and then say, "Right, you're done." Then I would go back to the train station and sometimes just miss my train and wait for a half-hour for the next train. I kind of got used to this, but during the winter months, it worsened. The cold weather, I believe, put people in a bad mood as they would often be a bit cranky in the Job Centre. I remember venting my frustration to a female member of their staff. She simply said, "Well, Carl, no one is holding a gun to your head and forcing you to come into the Job Centre," which was very true. I just smiled and said, "I know."

A whole year had passed, and I applied again to the Summer Camp I'd been to five years earlier. I had applied late, giving a three or four-week notice. Fortunately, the same Camp Director appeared delighted to have me back, and he recommended the YMCA as my sponsor. When I arrived, another Counsellor told me that I was mentioned in their staff meeting as someone to look up to and ask questions if in need. I never really thought of myself as the leader type, so it was nice hearing this.

This is where we had the Evening Opening Campfire, generally with a hundred kids and about forty staff members in attendance. Here, the children would be introduced to their camp counsellor and meet the other kids in their cabin. Safeguarding was imperative. Photographing the children was not allowed.

Soon after camp, I had spoken to my ole' Australian matey a.k.a "the African truck driver". He had said he had seen all the wonders of the world. I became a bit jealous, so I went online and booked an eighteen-day Oasis Overland Travel trip from Cairo, Egypt to Amman, Jordan departing within six days. Visiting two wonders of the world on this trip; the Pyramids of Giza and the Treachery in Petra, Jordan (a New Wonder).

JD = Jordanian Dollars

Patiently waiting for a hot air balloon ride.

September 2011- an Egyptian Desert, Luxor.

Photographed from a hot-air balloon with twenty or so people in a huge basket split into four. I paid only £75. Would I do it again? "Umm…. No!"

This was an amazing trip. The forty-eight-hour felucca (wooden outdoor sailboat) trip down the River Nile was utterly incredible, especially jumping into the Nile and swimming, pulling into the bank and eating delicious foods, and dancing around a small campfire after sunset. Needing to go for a number two wasn't much fun, as there were no toilets, so I just had to find a bush and go in the fields. I was given some toilet paper. I can vaguely remember hearing goats communicating nearby. Probably wondering, "Oi, who allowed him to offload in our field?"

After bartering for a bag of foreign crisps, the children went for a swim in the River Nile, and after our lunchtime, we continued on our felucca journey down the famous River Nile onto Aswan. Most of the group had not heard of Aswan. As mystical as it may sound to some, it's just another city in Egypt.

July 2010: The children swimming in the Nile River.

Aswan Abu Simbel - an astonishing sight.

This was incredible, and the etchings were enormous. I recall approaching this glorified hill from behind and not seeing much, but then I was amazed as we walked around to the front.

Wadi Rum Desert was amazing too, except for my middle of the night pee, which was a bit scary. Luckily, I didn't pee my pants. We stayed at a camp in the middle of the desert. While waiting for dinner, I saw around twenty children with different special needs, who all seemed a little agitated. I had spoken to their teachers and learned what they enjoy doing. I decided to teach them a dance I had made up with the kids at camp. It only lasted for about three minutes. After, I was surprised and wondered to myself, "Why am I so tired?"

It was such an amazing adventure holiday. I met a lovely French lady, Lauren, on the same trip, who suggested that I apply to work in the French Alps and work in the Chalets. It was to help practice my French, and you know what, I did. Another highlight for me was going to the Dead Sea as I remembered being told about this place years before. I could not believe there was a sea you can float in because of the high salt density. What was cool was that they had these huge tubs of Dead Sea mud, which you are meant to cover your body with before you go in.

*In a place called **Madaba**, I politely asked a hotel receptionist if I could go to the roof as I am a student and I need a **high vantage point, which you can see in the photo above.***

Stupidly, I thought at the time; it would be funny to submerge my head into the Dead Sea for ten seconds. I did, and it made most of the group laugh, though the others probably thought, "Oh, you idiot." I would not recommend it, as it is excruciating.

Just following this great adventure, I decided to apply for a job in the French Alps. Luckily, I got offered an online interview over the internet; how cushy was that? Straight from my own home with the large French company, Club Med. The interview lasted about an hour, and toward the end, I was asked when I could start. I thought briefly and said, "Tomorrow." Thinking she would say, "You don't have to start so soon," I was surprised when she said, "Okay, that's great, I will send you the tickets this evening with directions to the hotel and someone from the company will meet you tomorrow." The company was to pay for travel to and from home. By saying this one word – "Tomorrow," I had shown my eagerness to work, and I believe this cemented in her mind who to give the job to. I was employed as 'Un Animateur' (Children's Play Leader) and arrived at the four-star hotel in Serre Chevalier the following evening.

Very early on in this contract, while taking the skis for a morning session on a minor slope covered with snow, I tripped and fell down the slope and rolled to the bottom. I quite clearly remember an Italian saying, "Je crois qu'il l'a fait exprès", which means, "I think he did it on purpose." Everybody laughed, except me. It didn't hurt, but it amused people due to the way I landed. The laughter didn't bother me, but I certainly didn't do it on purpose. Not sure why anyone would do a thing like that.

I enjoyed the travel and the French-speaking I was getting practice with, but I was not sure why I was not keen on the white snow-covered mountains or the cold temperatures. This job was not too difficult. I can vaguely recall a time when I spoke to this plump chap. Then, shortly after, finding out he is a very famous comedian in Belgium; I hadn't heard of him. The first contract was only a week; at the time, this was okay. Now it might seem like a lot of hassle because by then I had getting on a bit. A week or two at home, and then off to 'Aime–La–Plagne' for a month. Still, I did not mind it at all.

January 2011 - Aime–La–Plagne

It was a nice experience going through the snowy mountains on the train and then taking the cable cars. Falling in the snow, which I did two or three times or more, was not painful. Stepping into about a foot of snow and watching my foot sink in, now that was a little crazy. I remember sitting in a balcony restaurant overlooking the mountains, with five of my French colleagues, eating pizza, which I did not order. A good French-speaking experience, though. Please be aware that some people lose their life skiing. It can be very painful if you fall in the wrong place, so always be vigilant when skiing.

Grenoble seemed like a lovely place, but I only got to pass through. One evening, when working in the French Alps with

Club Med, I was asked by a colleague around my age if I wanted to go to Meribel, basically to keep him company while he dropped his girlfriend off. I said, "pas de problem mon ami." "How long is the drive?" He responded that it would be around four or five hours. A little shocked, but knowing I could sleep in the next day, I went without hesitation.

I remember the day I arrived. My bed had a massive pile of dirty clothes on it that belonged to my roommate. He was a nice enough guy. One night, I remember how he desperately wanted me to sleep somewhere else as he thought he was going to get lucky with a girl. He even offered me 30 Euro to not come back to the room. I, of course, responded with "Non non, je ne pense pas alors." "No, no, I don't think so." One night he irritated me a little because he wouldn't be quiet about how I reminded him of a famous person. Twenty minutes had passed, and I was very nearly asleep and he said "Eh oh Carl, tu dors? Je souviens. Tu l'air comme Monsieur Bean!" "Carl, are you asleep? I remember. You look like Mr. Bean!" He was a young French guy from Paris. Albeit, I disagreed, I used to laugh a lot watching Mr. Bean, so I said nothing, just smiled.

We had to work six days a week there. Our job was predominately to look after the children. It entailed preparing them for their ski lessons in the mornings and afternoons, and picking the toddlers up from the children's' practice slopes, and reassuring them when they fell on the beginner slopes. We served them their lunches, played with them in a crèche, and had an occasional snowball fight. We also mingled with parents in the evening at the bar and nightclub. Sometimes we even boogied with them on the dance floor.

My time with Club Med was short-lived. Partly, this was due to not getting along with the manager, who was four-years-younger than me. I recall him sternly telling a team of about twenty-five staff members, "Il faut que tu travaille comme de robot." "It is necessary that you work like a robot." What a juvenile plonker! Not surprising at all, he was not a liked man. I will never know how he became a manager, probably because he was French and it was a French company.

On my travels home, I arrived at Lyon Airport around 1 A.M. My flight was due to depart at 06:30 A.M., five and a half hours later. I had been told a hotel would be around 100 Euros. So, I managed to find a deserted sofa to sleep on and uniquely positioned myself so I wouldn't be seen sleeping until my flight. Saving myself 100 Euros was worth it. Three years later, I was invited to an interview with Mark Warner, a British company, but very similar to Club Med. This time I did not attend that interview.

After that initial contract, three weeks later, Club Med got back to me regarding the evaluation. It was quite positive, but they did not want me to return for another contract. Fair enough, their loss, I thought.

The months passed by, and again, I could feel that I would soon be going crazy, talking to myself and my black cat Willow, looking at absolute rubbish on the internet I shouldn't be, as it was a clear waste of my time. I recall reminding myself daily not to waste my time looking at this stuff. Severe unemployment was bothering me; I became quite bitter towards Mum, especially. "I hate living here!" I would shout with gritted teeth.

Summer, 2011. I saw an adventure holiday I had to go for. Why, you ask? Because it was so cheap and I had always had an interest in that part of the world. It was Kathmandu, Nepal, to Delhi, India, including the Golden Triangle – Agra, Varanasi, and Delhi. So, I went.

The truck seemed a little old, and I recall during the first few days we were told it was built in 1984, the actual year I was born. The sixteen-day trip became an eight-day trip on the truck as it broke down on a dusty roadside. I think we waited at least an hour before being picked up in these tiny 4x4 Jeep-like vehicles. It was crazy as there was an Estonian couple on their honeymoon on this trip with us, a very friendly, adventurous couple.

The first day of the trip was mental. There was a British girl on the same trip, and I walked through Thamel, Kathmandu with its narrow streets, taking in the different smells and colours everywhere. There was very loud music playing, people selling pink candy flosses, lots were dancing, and getting henna tattoos. Someone told me it was Hare Krishna's birthday.

I bonded with everyone, but this time refused to go on the Whitewater Rafting trip, as being flipped three times on the River Nile wasn't much fun, even though I knew it would be going over grade-three rapids, which aren't as rough. I remember being in a kind of outdoor toilet of a bar/nightclub and sweating profusely. While sitting on the toilet, I could actually see drips of sweat falling off me due to the immense heat. Funny, I remember that. I suppose it was possibly my most uncomfortable time doing a number two in a loo.

We stayed in a treehouse campsite next to a river. It seemed quite up-market for where it was. We visited Jaipur's pink city, and even wearing my sandals, the floor was incredibly, painfully hot. I needed to spend a penny and saw a door ajar, so I pushed it open to find an elderly man squatting down doing his business. "Oops! So sorry!"

I recall staying in a one-star or half-star hotel and having to shower with just a sponge and a bucket of water. For dinner, I had ordered a plate of mild biryani at the roof restaurant, overlooking the city's hustle and bustle. Outside, people were selling from their food stools on the street just outside the hotel, and the constant beeping of car horns, something I heard daily in China, permeated the air.

I remember going to the River Ganges and being told that it is too dangerous to go on the river because it's monsoon season. The group went down to the river and watched near-naked people bathing in the sacred river. A few days later, we went to an area where three hundred people had just been cremated, and it was all out in the open. It was very bizarre, being so hot and having big white flakes fall on us, as though it was snowing. At first, I hadn't a clue what it was, but soon after found out that it was ash falling from the cremation.

August 2011, the River Ganges, Varanasi

A few days later, we were on the move again – this time to Agra (opening scene in Disney's Aladdin). I saw a chap leaving the three-star hotel we were to stay at for three nights, wearing a cool 'Kurta' or a 'man dress,' and I wanted one myself. The following day he picked me up from my hotel on his motorbike, and we went to his shop about five or ten minutes away. I bought three things from his shop; the guy was very good at bartering. In the end, we agreed on the price, and he took me back to the hotel. I haven't yet worn my Indian Kurta in England once. That was about seven years ago.

The following morning, we had to wake up early, around 5 A.M. to go and visit the **'Taj Mahal,'** which is, without a doubt, the most impressive man-made structure I have ever seen.

September 2011- The Taj Mahal

Its beauty is beyond words. Everyone was getting their photos taken with it, using the Taj as an impressive background. I think I may have sat on the bench that Princess Diana sat on approximately twenty years earlier. We next went on to see what was called 'Baby Taj,' a scaled-down version, which was also impressive to see.

The shot below is me in my man dress and the beautiful **Taj Mahal.** My Nan mistakenly thought I was Princess Diana; I think she needs her eyes checked.

September 2011- relaxing a few minutes and thinking about all I had seen in the North of India.

It was near the end of the short adventure, although I thoroughly enjoyed it. It was a huge eye-opener to see the severe poverty all across the North of India. It's very different seeing it with your own eyes, rather than on television, as it is just as easy to turn to another channel and almost pretend you hadn't seen it. During the last few days, I saw a stage show all in Punjabi; my friend and I didn't pay the extra money to have headphones with an English translation. The following few days after the trip I became quite ill, probably food poisoning again. I could barely go souvenir shopping for the family in a peculiar underground shopping place in Delhi. I remember on the taxi ride back, it was pouring rain, and while stopped at traffic lights, there was an extremely old man squatting knee-deep in a puddle of water. There is sadness like this everywhere, all over the world. You can make a difference and help, possibly by joining an overlanding group as I did.

I flew home while I was still suffering from my horrible illness. The flight was eleven-and-a-half hours from Delhi to London. This was quite possibly the worst flight of my life, and I haven't flown anywhere of great distance since; by myself anyway. That was my last overland trip. It turned out to be a Delhi Belly (food poisoning) I had caught, probably from an uncooked piece of chicken.

CHAPTER 8: DESPERATION SETS IN

I think another year passed of unemployment and signing on at the job centre and talking to my black cat, Willow.

Fortunately for me, toward the end of the year, I saw an online agency that Disneyland was recruiting in London, but it required a fixed-term for a CDD contract (a French thing). Because I knew I had a decent chance of getting a job as I had spent my Gap Year there, I applied, had the interview, and got offered the position from February 2012 – September 2012.

When I first entered the apartment with my two suitcases, a girl was doing something with her DVD player. She did not get up or even say hello to me. Indeed, not a warm, wonderful welcome. It turns out the roommates were British and in the Disney parade. One was Minnie, and the other, I think, was Pluto. Knowing I was super tidy and clean, they filled the sink with dirty dishes and left them for close to two weeks, hoping that I would go or just change apartments. At the time, I didn't realise their plan, although I was aware that they did not like me. Since we had different jobs, it was easy enough to ignore them. Just because I wasn't a young dancer in the Disney Parade, they chose not to like me. About ninety percent are British, and a high percentage of the males just want to play football on and off the pitch.

Backstage at the Village, I remember seeing Native American Indians while having lunch. They were cast members from the Wild West Show. At first, I thought it was a bit strange, seeing adult men with long braided ponytails down to their backsides, but after a little while, you can get used to seeing things you haven't seen before.

It was very different ten years earlier and my memory had faded. When I arrived, I was placed in the Plaids Residence.

Someone had made a mistake; I was supposed to be in La Bois-erie. It felt very bizarre at first, but I slowly adjusted to my sur-roundings once again.

Most of the people were in their early twenties or younger. One thing I did differently was that I washed my bed linen every three weeks. I was closer to the laundrette than in my previous positions. I must have been a right dirty bugger at eighteen. It was great to see some of the staff I had met before at Disney, some of whom began working for Disney in 1992 when the park first opened its doors to the public.

The job was very different, now that it was a five-star hotel, though it looked the same. I'm unsure how they were able to get that extra star. I worked in the Disney Village in a boutique called 'Planet Hollywood.' It was a pretty good job, and some people remembered me from my manure-sweeping days, which was crazy; I had only worked there for about five weeks, ten years earlier.

Disneyland Hotel

I decided during a morning work shift to do some yoga for the rest of the early starters. It was an idea to help put staff in a good mood for their day. It only lasted two days because I had no experience in teaching yoga and hadn't thought about the shapes, sizes, and ages of the other colleagues. But it's the thought that counts!

I learned **the importance of always being grateful** and surprisingly got free VIP passes because of it. A new member of the staff joined the team, who was just eighteen. I was Tara's assigned 'buddy' and recalled taking her to the park for the first time and seeing her amazement when coming upon the princess's castle. Unfortunately, this time, it did not wow me as it had ten years before. Also, many of the shifts at work were 6 P.M. to 2 A.M., so it became a tad tedious. Tara was a new cast member and as I was the only member of staff from England, I became her buddy to show her the ropes and have her shadow me and learn.

I didn't foresee this. One lunch with Tara, I told her about the Wild West Show, and the chap who played 'Buffalo Bill' from the show overheard our conversation and was very appreciative of us chatting about his show. He said that he had some free VIP passes for his American family, and we can have them because he won't use them. He then said they were in his room at home, and asked, "Where do you work?" I told him the boutique where I worked, and he said, "Well, I'll pop by in a few days from now and give them to you before a show." In all honesty, I didn't expect him to come and find me to give me these tickets as there were lots of boutiques in the village, but he did, dressed in all his attire, including the cowboy hat he wore in the show as 'Buffalo Bill,' one of the lead stars. I was a bit surprised to see him, and, of course, showed my gratitude. **See, those good manners and speaking positively go a very long way.**

I remember seeing the same sign on the back of the reception door in the Disney hotel for cast members. It read 'Smile and make someone happy.' It had probably been on the door since the beginning, twenty years earlier, in 1992.

This new guy joined the team, a twenty-one-year-old from Germany. During lunch one day I told him about my hard life and the crazy work hours we did on cruise ships. He asked me, "What was your average working time on ships?" I told him about ten-hours-a-day. He looked at me and said, "Well, what did you do for the other fourteen hours?" I was seven-years-older than he was, but he was right. In this day and age, too many people moan and complain about how hard their life is. When you stop, sit down, and think about the hours in the day, it may come as a shock how many of these hours are wasted. We only need seven or eight hours of sleep, and, of course, a little more if we are on medication.

My second week back at Disney, I was learning to operate the till, 'la caisse,' as it was known in France. I have fond memories of Luis, a guest, who had just bought something. I said, "Vous voulez paie comment?" "How would you like to pay?" Hesitantly, a few seconds later, he responded, "Cash!" My immediate thought was that it was rude to answer in English when it was as clear as crystal that I was a foreigner making an effort to speak French. The transaction was complete and he walked off. He came back to my till about two minutes later and said, "I live locally. Can you teach my two daughters English?" and gave me his business card. We arranged to meet days later and had coffee. He walked me to his gated apartment and we agreed on a price, and that was it. I found out the family had been looking for a woman English teacher for several months. In my two days off from Disney, I would go to the apartment and teach his daughters. Near my contract end, Luis drove me around to approximately seven or eight hotels with my translated CV, as his wife wanted me to stay; perhaps he did too. After my last class, I was invited to have dinner with the family – a lovely family with two adorable little girls.

One late evening after work, a very loyal, friendly, Portuguese Disney Village colleague told me that I came across as average compared to everyone else. Not that it matters; it definitely does not. What is normal, anyway? Is there even such a thing as normal?

I always found it quite bizarre when during our lunch breaks, each department always sat together and had lunch. The workers never sat with workers from another department. Well, I did a few times, but that is just me. **Being different is a good thing; it means you're unique.**

My Mum, Lee, and Nan came to visit midway through my contract time. They did the two Disney Parks all day, including the Tarzan show in Adventure Land, which I loved, especially the Phil Collins. Fortunately, Nan had her disabled badge, which meant we could go on many of the rides almost straight away. However, we were told a few times that the 'Pirates of the Caribbean Ride' was not open, and this disappointed Mum. At the end of our exhausting day, we headed back to the hotel and noticed the queue for the 'Pirates of the Caribbean' ride was filling up. A member of staff said yes, it had just opened. Finally, that was our last ride, Mum's favourite ride.

During their stay, we did a Paris open-top tour bus and got completely drenched in a torrential downpour but got back in time to see Disney's Twentieth Anniversary. There was a massive firework display and holograms forming certain Disney characters that were projected in the fountains and on the front of the castle using special lighting.

The following day we did the Wild West Show in Disneyland Village, which is a must see if you like "Cowboys and Indians". Their stay was spread over Friday, Saturday, Sunday, and they returned home on Monday. I have heard it's one of my Nan's favourite short breaks. I was obviously pleased they had such a nice time. Being a Disney cast member, I was able to get them a fifty-percent discount for the Disney Hotels, and two free entries to the park. I also had a very nice time but was exhausted, and the Monday they left I had to work a 6 P.M. to 2 A.M. shift.

During my second stint at Disney, I met this chap on the bus whom I recognized from before; we worked in the same hotel. He was very feminine and clearly gay. He invited me to his apartment, we got a pizza on the short walk to his humble abode, from what looked like an ice cream van. There was an oven inside, but not a fridge. It was a mobile pizza van. He didn't speak any English; it was to be a pleasant language exchange.

It started okay; he offered me a drink, and I requested something non-alcoholic. He told me that the drink was just fizzy peach without alcohol. He kept telling me to drink up and then he would refill my glass. Of course, I thought something seemed strange after the fifth drink. Suddenly, I thought I would scope out the kitchen. It turned out that the polite, friendly, gay guy was trying to get me drunk. It was getting late, so it was time for me to leave. In the final ten minutes, he told me about this new fancy underwear he had bought and wanted me to try them on for him. I just said something like, "Sorry, maybe next time, I have to go as it is getting late." The last thing he said to me was, "Montre moi ta bete," which means, "Show me your dick." I don't think so, so I stumbled home, which took about twenty minutes since I was quite tipsy.

The regular meet up with Mayte, my supervisor from the Disneyland Hotel, was always at this pastry store called 'La Brioche', inside the long thin shopping centre in Val d'Europe. There was a large Auchan, a grocery store I would go to once and sometimes twice a week. On one of my first visits, I was stopped by a staff member upon entry and asked to fill out a form to use the fast scanners – the plastic banana-shaped thingy. I would scan each item as I shopped; it became very useful because it meant I did not have to queue for long. Also, there was a beautiful piano in the centre and an underground aquarium in this shopping centre, which was unique. It led out to a chic Japanese-style outdoor section that had all the top clothing brands – Gucci, Prada, Louis Vuitton, D&G, and Armani. Then at the end of that, there was a children's play area. Mayte would sometimes come with her child, Alba, and we would walk through the swanky clothes section to get to the play area. The posh section outside was far too expensive for us to shop in.

Once again, I had lunch in a restaurant backstage, which was easily a third of the park's size, possibly even half the size of the park. After I stood up, I walked out of the staff restaurant and got the bus to exit the park. Once on the bus, I put my hand in my pocket and suddenly realised I had left my wallet in the restaurant. Good thing, at this point, I had a fairly decent level of French words built up. So, I was able to retrieve it; fortunately, someone had handed it in with the money still inside.

While writing this book, I have very fond memories of Disneyland. I'm sure these memories will stay with me forever. In Disney, I grew up a lot, gained confidence, learned another language, and learned to be more tolerant of people.

Since leaving China, I joined a language exchange site to improve my Mandarin and French, or at least not to forget what I had already learned. I met three Chinese girls in Paris through Conversation Exchange, an internet site, and once met a lovely Spanish girl from Sevilla on this site. Bizarrely, she was au-pairing (looking after children, 24/7) just up the road from me in England. We both had an interest in dance, so together, we attended the local Park Hall for a Ballroom and Latin dance class. I recall standing on her feet a few times; I wasn't as good as I thought I would be. She went home to Sevilla three days later, and that was it.

CHAPTER 9: BACK TO THE JOB HUNT

This time I had another Uncle helping me with my colourful CV. I soon got a job near Windsor Castle in a four-star hotel. The MacDonald Windsor Hotel – I worked in the Concierge Department alongside the front of the house. After my three-month probation period, they decided to extend it a month and then another month, but in the Housekeeping Department, where I struggled. It was very different from the Housekeeping Dept. at the Disneyland Hotel. I was getting noticeably slower to friends and some family, though I did not notice it at the time. To me, I was just a young twenty-eight-year-old.

I met a very well-dressed father and son. I asked them where they were going, and they replied, "Oh, just a party at Elton John's house." Okay! More like a mansion, I would imagine.

Scarily in this boutique-style hotel, I got stuck in a tiny lift with a guest around fifty-years-old and his luggage for one hour and ten minutes. All of my experience since age eighteen came in handy. I kept him talking; it was quite warm and stuffy that day, which made it worse. I managed to keep him reasonably calm, chatting, and smiling.

Another day, while on a break in a tiny narrow room with a fridge which was often empty, I saw on the wall that you could run the Windsor Half Marathon and the hotel would pay for your entry fee. Never really saw the point of running and paying for it myself, unless it started to rain.

I decided I would do it, so I joined the local running club, Burnham Joggers. On my first day, I remember telling someone that I used to run eight or nine miles per hour. They obviously realised I was telling porky pies (lies) when I ran five-hundred metres and felt like I was dying with a horrendous, painful stitch in my side. I did not know you shouldn't eat just before you go running. You should not eat for two or three hours before a run. I enjoyed running but started to be a little concerned with how often I would fall. Also, a slight toe fungus bothered me a bit as it spread across my entire big toenail. This was due to running in regular socks, not cushioned or absorbent running socks. The moisture from your sweaty feet causes the fungus. I attended a School of Podiatry for about a year, and they kept putting Tea Tree Oil on it, but there were no improvements. A neurologist in London's Charing Cross Hospital recommended using Amorolfine once a week; it's a fungal nail treatment which presently seems to be removing it. Apparently, it can take up to a year or more.

On one particular day during the Ascot Horse Race, I made £62 for doing an excellent job in one day, and that was extra. I can recall receiving three handwritten notes of recommendation by guests and a few more face-to-face compliments. Because of this, I was under the impression I was doing a good job.

Because I was in the Concierge Department, I was offered free tickets to see a West End musical. I hadn't heard of 'Once' and didn't know who to invite, even though I had requested three free tickets. All my close friends and family were working, so I decided to ask an Australian ballet dancer I had recently messaged on "Couch Surfing". She invited an Australian friend. We first met over lunch; both girls were very nice. Following lunch, we all walked together to the Phoenix Theatre; I can recall the two girls were constantly whistled at, most likely by builders; the arse crack eejits they are. 'Once' is a brilliant musical, and one we all enjoyed. One of my favourites, not far behind, is 'Blood Brothers,' another amazing musical.

The two younger female receptionists would always be talking behind my back, and I had spoken to their boss a few times. Their boss asked me to put all their maliciousness into writing. The girls received their warnings; they then suddenly appeared very nice to me. Obviously, they were afraid of losing their job. Then a couple of weeks passed, and I was asked to bring into the office this letter I had written about the girls, both who were in their early twenties. I did not bring in this letter as they were now extremely nice to me. Shortly after, they moved me to Housekeeping and then got rid of me. I was a little perplexed as I had two letters of recommendations posted on the board in the office, and I was regularly receiving tips. To me, this meant I must have been doing a good job. Hey hoe, life goes on. I felt it was their loss.

Months passed again, and I was unemployed for a while, signing on again for the Job Seekers Allowance or JSA as it was often known. I was looking for hotel jobs online; please remember I was pretty desperate. I saw a Sous Chef vacancy in the Ritz London; you know what? I sent a message to the PR person stating I had no experience in a kitchen, but my great grandfather was the Head Chef here for twenty-five years or more. They responded with, "Was your relation Jacque Viney?" Turned out my great grandfather had trained the Head Chef there today because indeed, he was Jacque Viney!

The Head Chef decided to give me a week's worth of work experience, I assume, based on that fortuitous fact. Rather than commute daily, I stayed in a nice hostel in Swiss Cottage, London, which was a short tube journey and a walk away. I shared a room with fourteen other people, all from different parts of the world. It was okay, though. I recall the minimum price for a room in the Ritz was £400 a night, which is a lot. In the Disneyland Hotel for the Presidential Suite, it was about 3250 Euro a night.

The job role was as a kitchen helper. Here I was asked to grate potatoes, sweet potatoes, artichokes, and zest lemons, which, at the time, I hadn't heard of zesting anything. I saw pastry chef's crack two eggs at once by delicately knocking them together. I was asked to wash some carrots just using the cold tap; my hands were in incredible pain from the freezing water. I was offered an eight ingredient Croque Monsieur that a guest didn't want, artichoke soup, and a delicious, slow-cooked duck egg. The duck egg looked transparent, something I have not seen before and most likely will never see again. On the last day, my Mother and an Uncle wanted me to get a photo with the Ritz's Head Chef. I did, reluctantly.

Soon after this very short work experience in The Ritz Hotel, London, I decided never to work in a kitchen. It is a very high-pressure job, certainly in a five-star hotel. I have always wanted to be a good cook, though. So far, the cheese on toast seems a little boring. I have learned to cook a Spanish Omelette and a Carbonara over the years as well. Not really difficult dishes.

So it was back to signing on (JSA) for a few more months and applying daily to find another job. I had a Skype interview with VCY (Village Camps Yorkshire) the year before, and they had offered me the job but I just wasn't sure I wanted to be in charge of a group of affluent kids bickering about who is the richest. I chose to go back to the underprivileged kids camp in Connecticut. Again, it was tough, like an emotional roller coaster. This time was different. I had thought I would see a few improvements, but I didn't. It was the same as it was five years earlier. It was harder sleeping in sleeping bags in these wooden huts and it got really hot and stuffy at night. When you're young, you don't think about things like that. I can remember jumping off a viaduct (bridge) with camp friends into a mini-lake; we were thirty-two-feet high. Only, before I jumped, I had forgotten about my mobile (cell phone) in my pocket. Also, when I jumped, my body tilted down, so I kind of belly-flopped and it hurt really badly. I had enough energy to doggy paddle to the side. Then I just watched my friends continuously jump in. About an hour before I had been on the phone to Mum in England, who had told me not to go. I did not listen, of course, and chose to be with my Kids Camp friends.

The following summer, I was offered the job at VCY (Village Camp Yorkshire) the affluent kid's camp. I was told when I could begin. I had to pay for the various trains to get where I needed to go. This time I was employed as a CELTA (Certificate in English

Language Teaching to Adults) Teacher. I had a fantastic time at this camp, and had the opportunity to teach in an old 1894 Victorian house, once owned by the Enid Blyton (English Author) family. I had read this on a plaque at the house entrance.

I went on a trip with the children to visit the old and new town in York. The old town was mainly all pebble stone and very quaint. I went on another trip to supervise the children and visited the Manchester City Football Stadium that was big and more known to those who lived in England. I was able to go to the Trafford Centre in the city of Manchester, which is the best shopping centre I have ever been to, even though I dislike shopping. All the staff and I went to play quasar together, which is a real-life indoor gun game, and once it was time to meet the children, we all went to see a Harry Potter film in the cinema.

I surprisingly enjoyed the Yorkshire Dungeons, as I vaguely remember being terrified of the London Dungeons. Now, at the age of twenty-six, I did not seem to scare at all. I do recall, in the Old Town, going into a store with an American friend from the Camp. The store was full of large fish tanks with humans sitting over the edge, dangling their feet in the water-filled tanks. At first, it did seem a bit weird. A staff member told us it is great because the fish bite all the dead skin off your feet, a good foot cleanser. I gave it a go, but it was so ticklish, it was hard for me to stop laughing. At this camp, as great as it was, the first week was all training. I got along well with everyone, but I suddenly realised I was extremely unfit as I had a horrible limp by the end of the week during the practice for fun camp games. I was given great work evaluations. In the last few days, something happened to me. I was walking away from the football field, and one of my legs suddenly locked up and did not bend as it normally would. I stumbled but luckily I didn't fall – still, it was a very strange happening.

I again thought to myself; I am still without a job. As it was headed into the summer months, I applied to the kid's camps again. This time it was with a different company that I hadn't heard of. The company was based in the UK, which meant I didn't need to fly. I was invited to the Camp Beaumont Recruitment Day. At the age of thirty, I assumed I would be one of the oldest, and as it was, I turned out to be the second oldest. I knew that I had a lot of camp experience, so I thought, what have I got to lose and just went for it.

Fortunately, because of my years of Kids Camp experience, I was offered the job. A few weeks went by, and we found out where we were going to – Bembridge on the Isle of Wight. I think this was the same camp my sister went to fifteen years earlier on a school trip; perhaps a little modernised now.

Every camp I have been to, there are different rules. At this camp, everyone had to wake themselves up. We still had to knock gently on their bedroom doors and tell them to wake up. Whereas, in other camps, we would encourage them to tidy their rooms and apply discipline if warranted.

The real cool thing about this camp was it was only a five-to-ten-minute walk from the beach, which had just one little shop on it. It was a nice quaint touch. I'm sure you can guess where all the staff went on their hours off, although summer in England is not always cool and hot. The weather can be unpredictable at times.

Day one of the Kids Camp tour

We went on a long **coastal walk to Sandown** two or three times, taking the children the scenic route, which was very enjoyable. On the last walk, though, just after mounting a small gate, there was a mild slope downward, and I sped up too quickly and threw myself to the ground just as I was heading for a ditch. I saw a Physiotherapist following the summer and found that because of the fall, I had damaged my rotator cuff which is a very painful shoulder injury.

Sandown Walk, Isle of Wight

I shared a room with a Spanish chap named Marcos. We got along well. I suppose that was because we were the second and third oldest. In most of my previous jobs, I have had to share a room with someone. It is alright, providing you get along.

One morning at the staff meeting, I was informed I was to go on a trip supervising the children to Amazon World, a zoo. I thoroughly enjoyed this trip, especially having two lemurs walking on my back, shoulders, and head. Unsure why they chose me, though I felt quite honoured. There were cool animals to see, South American parrots, quite a few meerkats, and huge, slow-moving tortoises.

The day we rented a car was cool; we drove from Shanklin to The Needles Headland and had a great time. We took the kids to a glass-making place near the Needles (three large rocks jutting out the water), which was also cool. I was so impressed with

The Needles. When we were with the children, we took a chair-lift over a cliff and down to a beach. The chairlift was similar to an outdoor cable car, but we were seated on a garden bench and strapped in for safety.

We would sometimes collect kids from the airport, and I once went on five modes of travel, all by midday – a bus, train, coach, taxi, and hovercraft. The hovercraft was pretty cool. The only hovercraft I knew of was the 'Toys R Us' hovercraft that very nearly sank in the central Black Park lake, Slough, when I was eleven or twelve. I recall looking at my watch, and it read 11:55 A.M.

Hovercraft – 3 times faster than the ferry.

One weekend, when I was able to have some time off, I went to an Art Exhibition to see my friend Zoe's photographic work and for coffee and a chat. She was a good friend from Reading College nine years earlier, and I have always liked her photography. I was pleased to receive an invite. She lives on the Isle of Wight.

Zoe Barker, currently on the Isle of Wight, has stuck one of her photos onto a red card, making it a Christmas card. Anyone can do this and perhaps even with a small drawing – just a money-saving idea.

The younger colleagues tried quite a few times to get me to go out drinking. I had stopped drinking at the age of twenty-one, so I rarely went. I did go to the staff party where the food was very tasty though. One of the party games was to give an honest opinion on who was the biggest drinker, the biggest flirt, hardest worker, most memorable, best bromance, most attractive, etc. among the staff. It was just a bit of fun.

I was given the award for the most memorable staff member, and Marcos and I won the awards for the best Bromance because we would occasionally bicker as couples often do. Though Marcos wasn't there, I really appreciated it and accepted the award.

Well, back to reality and another long period of unemployment ahead. A few people had started saying to me that my balance seemed to be worsening. I didn't notice. I went back to Burnham Joggers and fell again, this time severely twisting my ankle, leaving me unable to walk. This injury healed in about three to four weeks. I don't think that I was told this but just happened to read it in many of my hospital appointment letters but I had been diagnosed with Progressive Spinocerebellar Ataxia. Ataxia is an umbrella term for a group of conditions that affect balance, coordination, and speech.

Shortly after, a neurologist said that I should stop driving due to having absent attacks. My eyesight would blur for two to four seconds, which I knew could cause an accident on the road. The last thing I wanted to do was have a crash and injure someone or myself. I stopped driving in October 2015, which made things a lot harder for me because I had to walk everywhere or take public transport. Going to interviews that were of some distance was tiresome.

In the meantime, I started going to a weight gym five times a week. I paid for a year's membership in 2015. I decided to pay extra for a personal trainer for about five months to look better for my relaxing holiday with an Uncle. Approximately after two months, guys in the gym were making comments about my physique getting bigger. I felt a bit silly the day I was hunting for the 5kg dumbbells, and a female bodybuilder handed them to me. The dumbbell weight rack, I think, went up to 65kg, and the fives were the lightest on the rack. In approximately four months, to my surprise, I was able to double my strength in the weights' gym.

My Uncle, who is an experienced diver, and I went to Ranveli Village Island in the Maldives for ten days. We stayed in a three-star hotel and loved it. It was a tiny island in the Indian Ocean that was roughly twenty-to-twenty-five meters in diameter. The beaches were sublime, and I got to go on a seaplane for the first time. Every day my Uncle and I went snorkelling. He would go out on a diving boat, and occasionally I would go with him and snorkel; I was more than happy to do this. One day out with my Uncle, we saw about five turtles and two white-tip sharks all in the space of twenty minutes. A turtle came to the surface right in front of my face. It was amazing. I remember seeing a wall of fish under the pier. I looked at my Uncle nervously, and he pointed toward the wall of multi-coloured fish. All the fish just swam around me; I didn't even feel them. I loved it.

August 2015 - Ranveli Village Island

Upon returning home and telling everyone about this fascinating trip, I believe I started to look at nature differently, and I started to worry less. It was truly a wonderful feeling.

I also started going to the Charing Cross Hospital in London more and more, having MRI's and an EEG and various investigations. I even had a Sleep-Deprived EEG as the EEG scan was inconclusive. For this, I had to go to sleep after midnight, wake up at 3 A.M., then stay awake for the scan. The hope was that I would fall asleep for the second EEG scan. I didn't.

I met up with an old friend, Aoife, in Skerries, Ireland, who used to be a Radiographer in a Dublin hospital but one day decided to have a career change. She studied hard and did the relevant course to be a Personal Trainer. On the way home, I remember she told me she works fifteen hours a day, six days a week, to make ends meet. She was also younger than me. It got me to thinking that anything is possible.

The Namibian tour guide I had in Africa now runs his own tour company and is a local restaurant owner. When I was in Africa, I recall having been to his Mum's house in Namibia, so I know he is definitely not from a rich family. In the last two years, I have twice seen him in a selfie in Africa at some entrepreneurial fellowship with Barack Obama, the 44th American President, in the background. This strengthens my belief that anything is possible. You just have to try, and never give up trying.

"In 2011, I resigned from my job as a Tour Guide in Africa to pursue, what I called at the time, the Greatest Adventure of my life, which is to be a leading man of my time and not an Ordinary Citizen, but with the extra at the front.

In that period, I have built the Hafeni Tourism brand from scratch, and today, Hafeni Tourism is a brand the majority of Namibians can connect with, although we still have work to do.

In that process, I have realised that to be a leading man of my time; one needs to personally develop oneself and learn from best practices, nationally and internationally.

Today, I have various achievements such as a Certificate in Business from Wits University 2012, became the Chairman of the NCCI Swakopmund Business community and various community platforms, participated in Tourism Exchange programs in South Africa, and was part of the nine young leaders from Namibia Summer Scholarship in Saarland, Germany through GIZ 2013. I was also chosen as one of the young leaders to partake in the Mandela Washington Fellowship program in 2015; earned a Certificate in Business from Clark Atlanta University, and was inducted as a Leader in the Namibia Business Hall of Fame 2015.

In this process, I groomed myself mentally, intellectually, and proficiently to obtain this small achievement to inspire my generation through my story so, they too, can take a page.

Through God's grace, I move forward, and I remain grounded and humble in the process."

My friend, Heinrich Hafeni

It was days after my thirty-second birthday when I fell out of bed one night. Or that's what I was told. To this day, I don't remember what happened that night. I severely injured my leg, so much so that I was unable to walk down the stairs for the following three days. I had to go down step by step on my bum. I now walk at least five times slower than I used to, and I started to see a Neuro-Physiotherapist. One day, quite recently, she asked me to walk ten metres. I did it in 9.8 seconds. Straight after I said with a smile, "Usain Bolt runs 100 metres faster than I can walk ten metres." She laughed and said. "Everyone is different." **Being**

different is good, as it means you are unique.

I am much happier now, with my much-increased love for being alive, healthy, loving nature, animals, and people. I would like to feel stronger, but that will come in time.

I now believe all you need is to focus on one thing: work hard at it, be determined, persevere, and believe in yourself. Then, you can do anything. Thinking positively and healthy living are just as important emotionally and physically also. You should always have a goal in mind and always want to improve yourself.

Fortunately, my wonderful sister suggested I should try volunteering in my local area. I Googled it first, sent a few emails out, and made a few phone calls. Now I volunteer at a local youth centre in Burnham, just five minutes away on foot, so it is handy for super not-so-speedy me.

When I was younger, I used to wonder often, why I was here? Now I have a decent explanation of why. It is to help as many people as I can, wherever I go. Never stop smiling and being happy.

"Our Prime purpose in this life is to help others. And if you can't help them, at least don't hurt them." – Dalai Lama

To date, I have had a wonderful life; I've seen amazing things all over the world and have learned skills in abundance through travelling. I now cannot walk very quickly and have an unusual wobble (to some), which has some people assuming I am drunk. But I am still alive and can help people, smile at people, and spread my joy and happiness.

Remember, age is just a number; it doesn't matter how old you are. I had a lovely neighbour 'Joyce' who was 81-years-old, and she lost four stone (25kg) in two years just by cutting her calorie intake by half. I thought she looked great for it. This may not be possible for all, but you won't know if you don't try. We must try something and always remain positive for the future or cause tremendous family sadness.

Just one more thing. You do not need to be well-travelled to get a job in a travel company. You need to be pretty decent at Math and Geography and be very enthusiastic, driven, and personable (likeable). Show that you really want the job and how you can benefit their company. Sell yourself!

August 2007- Serengeti National Park. Notice the vulture on the tree.

How can you easily change your life to make it and others' better? It's not easy, of course. My grandfather once told me about finding work. If everything was easy, then everyone would have a job.

I see a Neuro Physiotherapist and a Neurologist who have both recommended swimming, yoga, and Tai Chi, which I now do weekly. I was having a Costa coffee with my niece, nephew, and Mum. Mum recognised this chap as he was the father of a child who went to my primary school. It was quite a strange way to meet, as they hadn't seen each other for about twenty years. He recommended I go to his Tai Chi beginner's class. Apparently, Tai Chi is great for those people with balance issues. I also do various floor exercises to strengthen my core muscles, such as planks, squats, push-ups, etc. All daily, and it does not take very long.

Through table tennis practice, I met a lovely Portuguese man who speaks French fluently, and by going to the Tai Chi class, I met a lovely Malaysian lady who speaks fluent Mandarin. Two languages I am currently learning – a bizarre coincidence.

I used to be a bitter person, full of hate, "Agh, I don't want to be an Uncle; I did not choose this!" It was my sister, who a few years ago, asked me to read a self-help book by Rhonda Bryne, *The Secret;* I think that's what the name of the book was. This book helped me understand more about appreciating life and the good things we have and significantly helped me to realise that there are many more people worse off, both physically and financially, than I am.

I recently decided to start thinking that everything is beautiful, waking at a decent hour, and loving all animals. I began to realise the importance of living, and this attitude has made my life more enjoyable, and I feel happier. Some might think this strange, as I still have my cool, unique wobble when I walk and walk slowly. Of course, nobody can know the truth here, but apparently, the mere chance of us being born is one billion to one. That is incredible.

After that, I read a few more self-help books, and amazingly, all of my bitterness slowly faded away. Weirdly, just like my verrucas. About five years ago, I had four to six verrucas on the soles of my feet. I went to a School of Podiatry once a month in Maidenhead. It was a pricey course, but cheap for the patients as, thanks to the NHS we did not have to pay. Of course, they were pleased to accept gratuities. One day I was there, and a lady told me how she had a patient who told her how all of her verrucas just vanished one day due to quitting her stressful job and living a happy lifestyle. I thought that was very strange. When I went to India, I would walk the soiled earth in old flip flops and sometimes barefoot. Once home, all the verrucas were gone. I do now believe it is linked to your happiness.

There was a day when I was in Ireland, visiting Dad. He asked me to watch an American movie, 'The Walk,' – a true story. I had heard about this film and probably wanted to see it at the cinema. I watched it and was left in utter amazement and shock – a wonderful well-made film, which I suppose prompted me to write this book.

It was about a Frenchman who had a dream, and his dream was to walk along a high wire between the twin towers in New York in 1974. I was born in 1984.

I remember having a dream and wanting to produce a great Photographic book one day, one that sold worldwide. That dream recently began when I changed my mind and decided to create this Photographic Self-Help book instead.

I try to get out and about. My sister has four kids I see twice monthly, apart from the once a week Tai Chi, yoga, swimming, and table tennis I do. Occasionally, I use the Conversation Exchange website to find a penfriend to practice my language with. I met a lovely lady from Belgium, born in Buccino Faso or somewhere near that part of Africa, and because my niece and nephews fight so much, I asked her if she fought with her three brothers growing up; perhaps thinking of being from a third world country, she wouldn't. She said, "Carl, tous les frère et des soeur bagarre de temps en temps, comme la langue et les dents." In English, "All brothers and sisters fight from time-to-time, like the tongue and teeth." I always remember that being a very good explanation.

One thing that irritates me is when children constantly

don't listen. If you don't listen, you are not going to learn, and that is "bu hao," "not good," for the world, or those around you.

Perhaps after one or two reads of this book, you may not see change. Change is something you can only do for yourself. My one hope for those readers is that it will make you think that change is possible. You just need to make an effort and try. I have found that travelling, especially in third world countries, will help open your mind when you see how impoverished people live, and this will hopefully sadden you into becoming a better person.

I had many jobs over the years, where I went to the interview but did not get the job. Even Matalan (a clothing store) paying five pounds an hour said I was unsuccessful.

I attended numerous primary schools, was employed by a good handful of travelling agencies, and I am well-travelled, but my Math was not up to standard. One travel consultant interviewed me in London. I was in a small room and asked to sit in front of this huge dog with pointy ears. Only afterward did I realise it was probably a test to see if I would stroke the dog; I did not. Although the interview went well, I did not get that job. A few hotels turned me away; actually, a three-star hotel in Maidenhead said I had too much experience. Sky Media said I looked too nervous. I volunteered in a Special Needs school, a new twenty-million-pound building (according to their head-teacher), from Monday to Friday for seven weeks. It was half-term (a week break), and I wanted to ask about my progress. I was shocked to find out they no longer wanted me back due to my poor balance, which I hadn't declared in their interview ten weeks before. So, they asked me not to return. I was a volunteer with Ataxia, and they turned me away. I remember thinking that it was very harsh, considering it is a SEN (Special Education Needs) school. I had heard that I was a great help, invaluable, and many other positives from the teachers. But due to my disability, which I hadn't declared, they did not want me to return.

When I was twenty-one at college, a classmate in his mid-thirties told me I'd make a great model. I went to one of the top modelling agencies in London and was politely told I have a great look, but I was an inch or two too short. I had interviewed twice with Disney Cruise Line and twice I was unsuccessful. My biggest upset was when I applied to be a photographer for the Royal Air Force (RAF). I was twenty-six when I first applied and was told that there were no jobs available. When I was twenty-nine, I received an email saying, "Please fill out the first stage of the application." Within a week, I received a congratulatory message, then one week after that, they said something like – "Sorry we cannot proceed with your application" – which would have been the first interview stage because it was three weeks short of my thirtieth birthday. This was their cut-off date, thirty-years-old.

Despite all the things I tried and did not get, I knew never to give up trying and never to dwell on the negatives. If you can't find a paid job, why not volunteer? It is free to help people and share a smile – it can make someone's day. Also, it can be gratifying when helping others.

In my mind, money is not that important. If you don't believe me, go on the Ultimate African Adventure with Acacia Africa and see how others live and survive with next to nothing.

Always remember, gratitude goes a long way, and anything is possible. You just need to try and believe in yourself.

I have not been intentionally trying to make my father seem like a horrible man and a rubbish father. We all make mistakes. He was, in fact, a great man. I have heard in the late 1970's he used to go voluntarily to the Canadian Red Cross Hospital in Taplow, Buckinghamshire, and offer his company to the children suffering from Rheumatoid Arthritis (RA). He is also very humorous and great with children. Just by talking to these children, he would make them forget about their aches and pains. Not a lot of people would do this.

Volunteer Appreciation Award
The Heart of the community

Carl Rooney

For your invaluable contribution as a volunteer at
burnham youth centre
Thank You for all your hard work! We couldn't of done it without you!

Chairman   _Club Leader_

November 2016

_"I am grateful for all my victories, but I am especially
grateful for my losses because they only made
me work harder." (Muhammad Ali)_

Just a few weeks ago, I joined a charity known as Sports-able, set up in 1975, and it allows people with various disabilities to play sports and be active. There are a good number of young volunteers that help, so it's helpful all round.

I do swimming and table tennis weekly with Sportsable, yoga with Mum on a Tuesday, and Tai Chi at noon on a Thursday. Friday evening, I am with Sportsable again practicing table tennis. I volunteer at a local youth centre on a Wednesday, supervising five-and six-year-olds.

We all have a talent and we all need to find our own path in life. It isn't easy, but it is near impossible if you don't make an effort and give it a go and try to find something you are good at and enjoy.

As I said right in the beginning of this book, I really believe if you wake up every day with a big stretch, arms and legs spread wide apart before you step out of bed, and then go to the bathroom and splash cold water on your face; this should hopefully set you on the right path to having a good day. I recently found out that cold water is actually very healthy.

I studied Photography, which is considered a "Mickey Mouse" subject by some. But do what you enjoy, not something your parents tell you to do. Learning about how the body works, perhaps doing Tai Chi or yoga, will improve your balance. A lot of people don't realise how important it is to look after their bodies. I certainly didn't. Everybody picks up bad habits throughout life, such as misusing their muscles, and it is important to know this, so later in life, you'll hopefully live longer and be stronger. Learning about nutrition and healthy eating is extremely important, along with a restful, good night's sleep.

I am not very flexible, and my balance is quite poor; a Neurologist recommended yoga to help with this. I love the humming exercises we do. To me, just listening is great; it sounds outer-worldly. We also do various breathing techniques, which I find a bit weird, but just by listening to your breath could perhaps help with sleep patterns. Give it a go!!

While I was with Burnham Joggers, on a few occasions, I ran through Cliveden House National Trust gardens. The first time was very tiring, but we came to rest at one of the most picturesque places overlooking the Chiltern Hills. I was mesmerised and shocked, as it was so close to home and I had not seen it before. I thoroughly enjoyed going back to that place, and the runs became easier each time.

CHAPTER 10: RANDOM IDEAS AND ONWARDS

Around this time, I thought it would be nice if we went out to a nice restaurant for breakfast on the first weekend of each month. It was something different for us to do, and it was nice to all have breakfast together, allowing us time to talk about whatever was on our minds.

I decided to design a photographic and travel ataxia website. People can easily see my photos and read about my photographic experiences, travels, and ataxia and how it feels to explore people and places that are foreign to you.

The idea was to boost and encourage, and let people understand that the world is a wonderful place, and it is important never to give up fighting whatever issues or various conditions or any other limitations you may have.

Earlier in the year, I decided to push ahead with another unique idea my sister and I had thought of many years before. Although I say 'push ahead,' I did not do much. I just asked my Facebook friends, "Does anyone know of someone who can draw?" I chose a photo, and Petra (an amazing artist) drew the other half. A reasonably easy idea that I really like. Unfortunately, nobody on eBay liked it, but I gained a friend from that simple Photo/Art idea.

One of the first rough practices for the Photo/Art idea

I had a nasty fall on concrete; I fell forward into a plank position. Since then, life has really changed. I walk, well, more like a hobble, and am a lot slower now. I was still practicing the front crawl (freestyle), a swimming stroke, with Sportsable, continuing with Tai Chi, finally putting my own idea into fruition. Earlier in the year, I thought up **CHOGA**. Tai chi and laughing yoga combined, Get it? Tai Chi and Laughing Yoga created CHOGA! I mentioned how we met a parent of a child from my primary school in COSTA who suggested I take up Tai Chi. Well it only took a few days of brainstorming after that and "Bob's your uncle, Fanny's your aunt" and CHOGA was born!

CHOGA - *tai chi and laughing yoga combined*

Email: ccrooney@hotmail.co.uk

A new exercise program for health and happiness

Improves physical and mental wellbeing

Supporting Ataxia UK www.ataxia.org.uk

Every Friday, 1-2 pm. Costs £3.   Starting Soon
Burnham Park Hall, Meeting Room 2

ATAXIA

Since the fall, a Neurophysiotherapist recommended Nordic Walking Poles, which I now use a lot; they help to support me when walking. They look quite similar to ski poles. Going down a snow-covered mountainside is not something I have ever enjoyed.

CHOGA was to be basic Tai Chi warm-up exercises and laughing yoga. When I went to get insurance, I was told I needed a qualification for laughing yoga. I was greatly puzzled by this. So, I repeated back what had been said just to be sure I fully understood. "You need to be qualified at laughing to make others laugh." Evidently, you did. I went ahead with the idea anyway, without insurance.

Later in this process, I hit another problem. I couldn't laugh for more than three seconds. I think due to a Dynamic Movement Orthosis (DMO) suit I had been wearing, which was supposed to help with my balance. It was very uncomfortable to wear. It was like a tight-fitted wetsuit. It was cool in the beginning; the medical staff spent forty-five minutes measuring me for the suit and then asked what colour I would like. It had to be blue with yellow stitching, but when asked, "Is there anything else you would like?" I jokingly had to request a large S and an orangey/red cape. Luckily, the man measuring me was my age and began to giggle; hence he saw the funny side. Mum, who was with me, asked, "What did the S mean?" Superman, of course!!

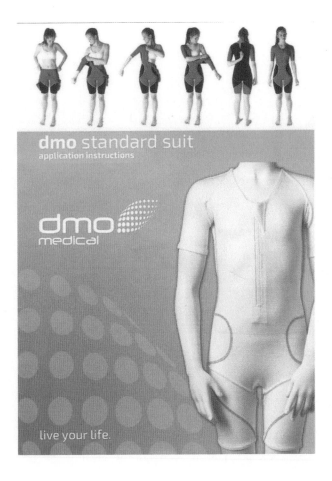

I had a minor issue within the first week of wearing it. I fell twice, and it hurt. Quite quickly after, I knew I had to forget the superhero nonsense. It was just a thin, tight-fitting wet suit that you couldn't get wet, also known as a Lycra suit. I decided to go ahead with the CHOGA class idea anyway. I arrived at the first-class twenty minutes early and set up with a few leaflets, unsure why, though. I suddenly had the nervous "number twos" but I still thought I had time.

When I went into the cubicle, I slowly got halfway out of the Orthosis, did my business, began cleaning, and then all of a sudden, all the lights went out. I immediately stood up, obviously holding whatever I could find, hoping it would activate the lights. It didn't. Somehow, I don't know how, I managed to finish wiping in the pitch-black room, as the cubicle was set back from the main entrance door. As I stood up ten minutes later, the lights came on. I pulled the tight wet suit back on and washed my hands as quickly as possible, knowing I was already ten minutes late. I went to begin the first CHOGA class. As I pushed open the door and went into the room, nobody was there. No-one.

I didn't give up. I decided to go back the following two weeks in the hope that somebody might turn up. The following week, four ladies were waiting to find out more about CHOGA. They were all willing to give it a go and were interested in finding out more about me and how the idea for CHOGA had started.

My main concern was not being able to laugh for a reasonable duration of time. I used YouTube and searched 'Laughter Yoga' to aid with this concern. There was a decent list of others who had arranged their own laughter clubs worldwide also. I still firmly believe that laughing can make everyone happier, and apparently, there are more than six thousand laughter yoga clubs worldwide and steadily rising.

My life has positively changed in a very good way. I began

saying I was housebound, which wasn't true as I had Mum and her partner Lee to give me lifts to yoga, Tai Chi, swimming, and table tennis, and when the occasion warranted, the bank and the hairdresser. However, I didn't like asking because they would have to take time away from work.

In September of 2017, I noticed my speech started slowly worsening. It became more challenging for me to speak, so I spoke less. A Neurologist claimed I slurred more, and apparently, it had become a little nasal sounding, too. It didn't matter, but looking back, I used to be a shy kid. As I became more confident, I spoke a lot more, and now, because of this neurological condition (that I had no idea I had), I spoke a lot less again. I just knew that life goes on, and many other people are far worse off than I was. I requested a Neurologist to refer me to a Speech and Language therapist.

I decided to send out a leaflet entitled "Would you like a FREE portrait?" I gave it to eight neighbours. Within two weeks, I received a phone call from one of the neighbours requesting portraits for their website. I was delighted to be able to photograph near home. At the photographic end, they surprised me with, "How much do we owe you?" I insisted it was a FREE portrait; money was therefore not required.

A regular trip to Ireland was booked on Aer Lingus, a visit to see Dad, family, and friends. When booking online, I opted for disability access, not realising I would be asked to sit in a wheelchair, which was an experience in itself. I actually felt bad shortcutting all of the queues and going through the Priority Boarding gates; I am no-one special, not a VIP. There is always a first time for everything, I suppose.

It was early January, and the Sportsable swim coach messaged me to join in with a swim challenge at the Magnet Leisure Centre in Maidenhead with only three days notice. I thought nothing of it and instantly replied, 'Yes, okay.' It was to be a Swimathon. I hadn't a clue what it was; I just thought they would tell me when I got there. On the day, I had changed, got my Nordic walking poles and hobbled out to the pool. I didn't realise parents were also invited. As I slowly walked around the pool, I suddenly stopped, looked to my left, and said, "Hello." Theresa May (the second woman in British history to be Prime Minister) was standing just over a metre away and replied, "Hello, enjoy your swim." I had seen her many times on TV before that moment; she just struck me as being very pleasant. A strange happening.

A few months after this incident, I was informed by the Sportsable swimming coach that I was invited to attend the award ceremony coming up. I had received an email a few days earlier and deleted it, as I wasn't overly keen on the menu. Sportsable gave Mum a call; Mum informed me that we were going. I was pleasantly surprised as I won two awards – one for progress in swimming and the Best Endeavour Award. Being as tired as I was, I had seated myself at the back of the hall. Fortunately, they were able to bring the awards to me because I could barely stand up, let alone walk all the way forward to collect the award.

I fall more often now, but I get up and soon forget about what just happened. I think life is a lot easier than people think. I hope this book becomes useful and life-changing to those who read it. We all need to love each other more and see everything as beautiful. If you stop and think about it, we all came from _one_ couple. Remember, there are twenty-four hours in a day, so if you think you are busy, just how busy?

I continued Tai Chi, yoga, swimming, and table tennis (the Chinese call it Ping Pang). I started playing the guitar following my daily morning exercises, which are normally the plank, push-ups, and leg raises. I might also soon be starting kayaking, though I am not sure; Sportsable has short-listed me.

I keep up with the languages: French, Mandarin, and Spanish, which has become a little challenging, as even English is becoming harder to speak now.

I move slowly around the house, usually going from door frame to door frame like Spiderman, so as not to fall over. I climb the stairs very slowly, especially in the evening, getting slower as the day goes by, a bit like the film *Everest* which occasionally pops up in my head. I have recently been working with a Language and Speech Therapist, and on her first day, she got me to read a paragraph and said it was, "like the fish mimicking a whale in the film Finding Dory", to help my speaking and make it flow a lot better".

Life goes on for me; despite being diagnosed, life slowly improved. I began to see things differently, became more positive, far more thankful than I had been. I started loving nature and animals a lot more than before. I became more tolerant of people, and I guess you could say, happy.

As I grew up, I would often hear that life is too short and time flies by. When you are happy, relaxing on holiday certainly does fly by. In general, for me, it definitely doesn't.

Back in 2005, I worked at Channel Kids Camp with a very athletic girl. I was quite surprised, about seven years later, to find my old friend Christa, the girl below. I thought I would just ask since my nine-year-old niece wanted to learn the trapeze:

Hey, Christa, have you seen the film *The Greatest Showman*? Did you like it?

I was in it! I was Zendaya's aerial double. Loved making it and enjoyed watching it. ☺

Zendaya plays the lead aerialist in the 2017 film *The Greatest Showman*.

My nine-year-old niece wants to be a Trapeze Artist now. All the family loved it, especially my niece. It must have been a great film to be a part of.

It was a pretty magical 5 months.

I am very happy I met her. She truly is a lovely person. We met when she had just finished school, a time when she was unknown as an amazing trapeze artist. She definitely stood out to me as being liked by all at camp.

Many people believe everything happens for a reason; that everyone's life is mapped out before they are born. But I don't. I can't quite understand this one. Things are not always able to be understood, but it does not matter if you think otherwise, as everyone has their own opinion about this.

People come and go in your life, as in everyone's life. I have had one main hairdresser for about nine years now. In that time, she has moved to another house, had a baby, and therefore knows that one day she'll move on and either I will find another person to cut my hair or I will go bald and not need a haircut!

I think I was about sixteen-years-old and sat waiting at the local Health Centre with a very old lady sat next to me and a youngish skinhead sat on the other side, near to her. I was raised to think those people who have these haircuts are bad news. But when this old lady stood up, and the skinhead chap helped her to put on a cardigan, I realised that listening to your parents is not always the right thing to do, especially in your late teenage years.

Life should be about 'WE' and certainly not 'ME' all of the time. It's this very thing that makes people unhappy, starting arguments about nothing or causing family breakdowns over nothing. One of the noblest things anyone can do in life is to help others. If we all try to have more nothingness inside of us, we will slowly become happier people and better people.

Using phones, the internet, and watching TV all create a very bad thing. Why do so many people just comfortably sit watching TV show repeats? This is something that baffles me; I guess I will never know why. I have heard they're linked to mental health. Stopping these usages and reading a nonfiction book or a novel will make you happier too, and more knowledgeable.

Another sad thing is people do not smile enough. If you smile at somebody, there is a good chance they will smile back at you. It is such a simple gesture that appears to be fading away. Please do not allow this to happen. Smile and make someone happy today. Even if it is you looking at your own reflection in a mirror.

It's now June 2018, and I, as you know, have Ataxia. I was recently told by a lady with Parkinson's, "You are my hero." She said it twice. Apparently, I gave her confidence when I swam, which was very humbling and nice, but a little strange because I am not sure how I did it. Maybe it was when I was younger and had a decent technique when I swam the breaststroke?

There are too many strange, weird, or bizarre things happening in the world. It is literally impossible to mention all of them. While at Kids Camp on the Isle of Wight, an eight-year-old girl accidentally swallowed a pound. When lying on her back on the grass, she had been playing catch; she didn't intend to throw it near her mouth. Oh well, she probably pooped it out later. Everyone has accidents in life. Just be grateful for any help received and then forget about it.

As time goes by, day-by-day, we will all get old and fall asleep and not awaken. It happens to us all. I never realised that in my youth, but now I think it is important to help as many people grow and enjoy living life as humanly possible before you pass on.

I have no idea why? I am thirty-four today, and the other day I got a letter through the post. I read on the A4 piece of paper, "A clean home is a healthy home." In the average home, over two million dust mites feed on dead skin scales. They hide in your carpet, upholstery, curtains, mattresses, and pillows. Mites can double their numbers in ten hours, and they can produce ten to twenty faeces a day. Why were we not informed of this at school? I guess I will never know.

Every single day upon waking up, you should feel glad for being alive. If you're dead, you're not much help to anyone. So being aware of your breath is also very important. Breathe in slowly, then breathe out slowly.

A lot of people may think you have to be rich to travel. Not if you volunteer as an English teacher in Malawi, Africa, or work in a bar in Mexico City and get paid while learning Spanish to make life easier communicating. In England, an affluent nation, for the most part, there is a lot you can learn about other cultures, and I do believe that this will help you become a far nicer person. Some companies pay for your travel abroad for work, although you are probably subtly subsidising this in your monthly wages.

I wonder why people always want more. Even at the end of a Connecticut Kids Camp, while building a fire, the excitement to collect more wood to make the fire bigger was crazy. Especially with money and power. This is an unhealthy trait. What's the difference between a Fiesta and Rolls Royce? Both are cars that drive and take you from point A to point B. One looks better and is, therefore, more expensive. But how important are looks; everything, including us, gets old?

Two days ago, I capsized while learning to kayak on Taplow Lake. It felt very strange as previously I could feel when I was wobbling in the kayak. This time I didn't feel anything and just went straight in like a duck fishing (I had been spotted going in headfirst), although I didn't see any fish. It happened suddenly, and I was, of course, wearing a life jacket, so the swimming was minimal. At the time, I was with a group from Sportsable, so I was around a fair, few qualified instructors who towed me back in the boat. I must have pushed myself too hard, or perhaps I was too eager to learn quickly. I won't even attempt to go around the lake next time.

About an hour ago in the garden, I saw a wonderful butterfly and thought, "Wow, you are so beautiful, but your life-span is just two to three weeks. I wonder how you live your life in comparison to how we live ours?"

It is so easy to forget that every one of us is different – every baby, every teenager, every adult, and even identical twins. It makes us all unique and beautiful in our own ways.

A very well-travelled friend of mine said to me once in Hong Kong, "You cannot help everyone," or something like that anyway. A couple of years later, I thought about it and had to agree, but I did think, well, you can help as many people as humanly possible before you pass on.

While looking over old photos for this book, I find it a bit strange that I don't remember any of them being taken. But yet, I am still in the photos. Your memory indeed fades as you age.

An amazing Uncle once informed me, "I'm not morbidly obese; I'm calorifically challenged." I say you are who you are. Nothing can change what's on your mind.

Every place on earth is unique in its own way. We can make positive changes and make the world a better place for future generations. I hope this book reaches out to millions of readers and hope it helps everyone who reads it.

We all come and go, be that to work, on a school run, and perhaps on holiday. A fifteen-year-old told me in brief yesterday about her family's stressful life. I couldn't understand how she had stress in her life, and apparently, it was because of her mock GCSE exams, but she's just a child, strange, huh? Someone should concentrate on exams being less stressful for children.

You know only one doctor over a landline call has ever told me "you have had this Ataxia condition from birth". It may be true or may not be true. At least I now know that it doesn't matter. A tad strange, I didn't even know about it until I was twenty-nine-years-old. We learn new things every day, and quite often, we do not even realise it.

I was holidaying with another Uncle who said something I had never thought of. Many set a morning alarm to wake you up bright and early for work, and some continue hitting the snooze button. My Uncle said, "why not leave your phone on charge at the end of your bed, forcing you to get out of bed to switch off the alarm and charge your phone at the same time? From there, open your bedroom curtains." I was thirty-one when I began doing that. It makes a lot of sense to me. Also, something I should have learned myself.

It is difficult to know the right path in life. When you are a child, you follow your parents, and you think everything they say is correct. When you're in your late teenage years, you follow no one and often get into trouble. Then, when you are a young adult, you're either travelling the world, attending a University, or hanging around with your friends, doing nothing.

One thing I have always thought is very odd is how people in work placements stick together. When I was at school, to get fit just before meeting the army careers advisor, I mentioned previously that I joined the school rugby team and suddenly gained a surprising amount of respect from my fellow year mates who played rugby. In gyms, for example, people hang in groups when working out. Suppose I was a unique floater.

Despite this dramatic change in my life, from travelling the world to being housebound with Cerebellar Ataxia – I live with positive people who help me massively. I guess it gives me the strength to be positive and stay optimistic for the future, believing there will be change.

If you do not share this opinion with me, it really does not matter. But being positive and having a belief is very important. Certainly, those people, be it family or friends, are very important. A few years ago, I went daily to a weights gym and slowly got physically stronger. After recommending this gym to a colleague, he immediately said, "No, if I were to go, when I strengthen myself, everyone will ask me to carry their household stuff." I hadn't even thought about this; as surprised I was, I am not one to argue. Fair enough!

As the years pass by, I am glad I can still laugh and smile. Having had a sore elbow gradually getting worse, I saw a local doctor about this irritation that comes and goes. She said, "You have golfer's elbow." Slightly unusual, I thought, as I have never played golf. Apparently, it's just a name. Anyway, I booked in to see a Physiotherapist.

It is what it is, Ataxia, or something else; life goes on. We are all very lucky to be given a life in the first place.

A lovely lady from Conversation Exchange wrote this to me:

"Hello Carl,

I'm Silvia. I would love to chat with you. I was diagnosed with another neurological illness. Don't worry, at the beginning you feel bad, but you have to think you can, and you aren't alone. If you feel like speaking to me, I would be delighted to chat. I am also interested in improving my English, and I can help you with your Spanish. Nice to meet you! Thank you."

"I've been thinking a lot about you. In fact, I started a Spanish teacher course because you inspired me. But when I had a week to finish the course, I got sick. I hope to finish it someday."

Many people from the Conversation Exchange website said they envy me after hearing about my travels. At the end of these Skype calls, I would often think it's effortless to book a flight online these days; it only takes a few minutes. Should you choose to work abroad, it's best to arrange an online job before you go.

My yoga class was great. With Mum at my side, we may always remember while lying on our backs the teacher telling us to do "cactus arms." This happened in every yoga class.

I recall my Tai Chi teacher saying, "Disease; many people misuse their own bodies over time, a dis 'ease' of the body. Throughout life, we all pick up bad habits. With your own patience, Tai Chi will amend some of these habits. Also, listening to Buddhist chants can be very soothing."

"There is more to life than increasing speed". (Mahatma Ghandi)

I remember when I was a young eighteen-year-old in Paris and having to perform a dance and surreptitiously staring at this hot choreographer's curvy rear end. Ten years later, in 2012, I ended up bumping into this same dancer while out shopping in Auchan. She was still beautiful; by this stage, she was married and had a child.

I can recall sitting on a bench in Serris Val d'Europe (shopping centre) and watching a lady in her seventies asking a little girl to move as she is young and doesn't need to be sitting down at her age. She was about two or three-years-old. I was left shocked; you cannot do that.

About eight years following the cruise ship job, I was on a train from Maidenhead. I recognised the voice of the guy behind me. I was about to get up to alight the train; it was a chap I knew from working on the *Jewel of the Seas*. Weird huh?

CHAPTER 11: RECENT TIMES

Mum and Lee decided a couple of years ago that we should move to Bournemouth in order to support my single-mum sister and her four children. I thought this was a great idea too, as living by the seaside is quite appealing, particularly when you've lived near Slough your whole life. So, after a few false starts, five months ago we left Burnham and moved lock, stock and barrel down to Bournemouth on the Dorset coast. Mum became my full time carer which confused me greatly as I knew she wasn't exactly qualified. However, overtime I realised that as long as you are loved and cared for then you'll be alright. Either that or I was encouraged to remember how Mum cradled me as a growing baby in her stomach!

I became slightly agitated about how clever the body's healing system is, except apparently when it comes to the brain. In a neurology clinic, in London I asked a senior doctor to roughly draw the brain and indicate the location, I knew it was at the back of the cerebellum (Latin for small brain) which controls co-ordination, balance and motor skills which can also seriously affect speech, as in my case. I was surprised by how small it was and wondered what the rest of the brain did. The funny thing is, I believe you can always improve but you just might not see your improvements.

My amazing Aunty Ann in Ireland sent me some exercise equipment, SmoveyMed. It comprises two tubular spiral hoops with a few ball bearings inside that when moved up and down in a sort of juggling motion set up a vibration that activates both surface and deep muscles, and stimulates the nervous system. They have been scientifically proven to help with Parkinson disease and my Aunty was hoping they might help me. Two of the easiest things in the world are to be nice and kind.....wouldn't it be nice to see more of this?

While waiting for the house move to be nearer Sis, the sea and to have a bedroom downstairs, I slipped on an old household rug which should have been attached to the floor. Because of my condition I fell flat on my face and heard my two front teeth break in half. Ouch! Thankfully, Mum was at home and an ambulance arrived which set me on the path for a temporary fix. I had to wait nine months to get my teeth properly fixed.

My nasally, slurry, slow voice is my voice these days, no one can understand me except those close to me who lean in and really want to listen. My balance has worsened over the years, so much so if I stand, I fall. This is why I am very grateful for a wheelchair and a 'Speaking Assistant' mobile phone app. I no longer need to stand. Did you know we have about 42 facial muscles and I fortunately still have a great smile. We all should concentrate on what we have and what we can do and keep smiling. A medical professional recently asked how I cope. I replied there are many millions far worse off than me and of course I am so lucky to have amazing family support.

After having spent a year and a half in a wheelchair, it was very strange when three months ago I had my first lesson with Dave, a physiotherapist. For me he is like a humorous magician and his best trick was to get me walking again. I said to Dave, "I feel like the giant in the BFG!", as suddenly I was viewing everything from up high again. The BFG is a Roald Dahl book and Steven Spielberg film about a Big Friendly Giant. Dave taught me to focus on my posture and slow movements in order to be able to walk effectively. Now Mum and Lee assist me and I am getting on ok. It is imperative to exercise to maintain muscle strength and this can be achieved while standing or sitting. I have heard various pieces of exercise advice such as, brushing your teeth using the other hand, standing on one leg or eating your meals with the fork (or chopsticks – kuai zi in Mandarin) in your other hand. It isn't easy, just keep trying. Apart from my slow movements. I can get by with the little upper body strength I have. I use both hands to form the letter T, meaning toilet. I can put two hands together to make a pillow showing I am sleepy and I rub them together to ask for a napkin. It seems to me I say "Ank ou" (thank you) too much but that may just be my slow speech. I point a lot at objects to explain things, mostly I enjoy giving thumbs up to express how I feel.

I mentioned earlier that I had treatment for an ugly fungal infection in my big toenail. I honestly thought it would never get better but after a young Bournemouth doctor prescribed me a simple tablet it did. It now looks just as perfect as my other big toenail. Whatever you have, whether it's a toenail fungal infection or Ataxia, I believe it isn't something you should let affect your life in a negative way. I have learned that being positive is everything.

EPILOGUE

I hope that reading this book has helped you in some way or another. Through either the words or the photos, I hope it has given you an idea of what you could do, be it helping as a nurse in a hospital in this country; volunteering in an elephant orphanage in Northern Thailand; or studying to be a veterinarian in the USA. Whatever it may be, try to do something you enjoy.

Never forget that if you go somewhere on holiday and have a great time, bizarrely, time speeds up. The expression time flies when you're having fun is very true. As I had seven years of fun travelling, coming back home to live with Mum was very challenging. For years, I hated being in the same place for a long duration of time, and not finding a job seriously dented my confidence and made things a lot worse.

Quirky Mum is often incredibly irritating. She is forever losing her keys, phone, glasses, and then dares to get everyone to look for her belongings. Mum has terrible listening skills and is awful with timing and prioritising things of importance. Bizarrely, Mum's fascination with looking at herself is very peculiar because it happens every day, and she always looks the same. We need only to remember all the good things she does. It may not be easy. It certainly wasn't for me, but with time, it will improve; it always does.

Family is very important, cleaning the floor daily, and the sofa weekly isn't necessary. Something I find marvellous is how Mum or Lee understand my slow, slurred, nasally speech, even when I cannot understand myself.

My sister and I mastered the art of laughter, which is said to be the best medicine. I feel so lucky to be born into this family. I also know that everyone is an individual, so it doesn't really matter if you're not in a loving, caring family; we all make a difference anyway.

I know that I have been immensely annoying to some people, even at times I wasn't aware of it. No one is perfect.

I would like to say, if you yourself have or you know someone who suffers from Borderline Personality Disorder or just BPD (not the Boston Police Department) or a mental health condition, I highly recommend this YouTube channel: Recovery Mum and if you would like to know more about me then search for www.photraxia.com

Something I suppose I will never understand is how the weather can change people's mood so dramatically. I just think if it rains, it rains; there is not a lot I can do about it raining. I would never get in a bad mood over it or become grumpy.

The following are a few guidelines for living that I have followed and that I encourage you to do:

- My neurologist said I have Cerebellar Ataxia, which medically is incurable, but some people recommend nutrition and lifestyle to reverse some issues you may face. It has to be worth a try!!
- Just know that there are millions of people in the world who may be worse off than you. Irrespective of the way we look, be nice.
- I think if we all keep smiling, being happy, polite and kind to one another, we might just get better. At least we will feel better.
- It matters very little about your condition. Whatever it is, through positivity and showing love and happiness for being alive, you'll do fine.
- Remember to be nice, kind, and considerate to everyone you meet; keep trying, smiling, and laughing. Make sure to always believe in yourself.
- The chance of us just being here is very slim; we may as well keep smiling and be happy. If smiling

is hard, pull a funny face in front of the mirror at yourself, or have someone tickle your feet.
- No matter what age you are, make sure you always to have an interest in something. That something can be anything. Try to always look on the bright side and be happy.
- Or you could learn to play an instrument.

I recall hearing on LBC, the London based radio station, that there are approximately 1.2 billion people on Earth with a disability. It saddens me to even think about it. One should always remember that there is someone in this world worse off than you are.

The adventures I have experienced, both at home and abroad, have made it profoundly easier to cope with life in spite of my own hidden disability. It is no longer hidden, and I couldn't give a sun-dried tomato what others may or may not think of me, nor should any of you.

Thank you very much for reading this; it is much appreciated.

*November 2003- Burnham Station. Three of my favourite
6x4 inch photographs from college.*

Special thanks to my Uncle James, Uncle Phil and Lee for your creativity, continuous encouragement and ongoing love and support

AFTERWORD

Although on the surface, this might seem to be an autobiography of an unknown person, it isn't meant to be. However, it is a true story from an unknown, non-famous guy, who hopes that viewing what has happened in my life will hopefully offer help to others in various ways. I hope that through humorous words and sublime photos it will give you ideas for unusual jobs and volunteering opportunities you may not have thought of before. Some of the not-so-great photos bring you along on my journey so far and add to this book's authenticity. All the photos, including the front cover (in Honduras) were taken by me, the writer, except those with me in them.

Reading it may even possess you to become an avid traveller, like me!

Remember this: You shouldn't look at old photos or dwell on the past as you have nothing to gain from it. Just know you can change your mind in less than a minute.

"Enjoying what you do is success itself – coming in first is just a bonus. Joy is the key." (Jeremy Vine).

THE END

Through a window. Your journey of life goes on.

Printed in Great Britain
by Amazon

86813203R00100